"A touching testimonial for animal lovers who've experienced deep connections with their pets"
—*Kirkus Reviews*

"This beautiful memoir confirmed what I have always known in my heart; that our spiritual bond with our pets cannot be broken… EVER! They will always be with us, comforting us, guiding us, and eventually meeting us in a better place. Having experienced similar spiritual events with my pets, I feel that animals are more sensitive, kind, and loving than humans can ever hope to be. An experience like this can happen to anyone if their eyes and heart are open."
—Sandy S., teacher, Pilates instructor, animal lover

"I loved this book. It is a wonderful story of love, hope, heartbreak and faith—a page-turner from beginning to end. Each chapter is filled with humor, surprises, and poignant dialogue. I was totally engaged throughout the book and gained insight into the life of dogs and the people they profoundly affect. As a cancer survivor I could relate to all the hardships, stress, and suffering chronicled here. However despite this, the book is uplifting and it will make you believe and realize that the power of love lives on."
—Mary-Ellen Marmo, Educator and Director of the Memteach Tutoring Agency

"Once in a while a book comes along that is a bittersweet miracle. Margo Bowblis' debut memoir is a treasure, an opportunity to share her wisdom and experience gained through the unforgettable journey and inspiring story of the life and death of Zeak, a very special dog."
—Doreen Corsetto, retired Library Media Specialist & District Supervisor, currently adjunct professor at William Paterson University

"Here is a thought-provoking story for anyone who loves animals. Whether or not you are a believer is irrelevant—you will be caught up in the "tails" that unfold. This wonderful book will bring smiles and tears to all readers of all ages who open their hearts and minds."
—Nancy Bosch, School Library Media Specialist

Walking with the Shadow of Love

The Remarkable Story of Lakota and the Zeakie Dog

Margo Bowblis

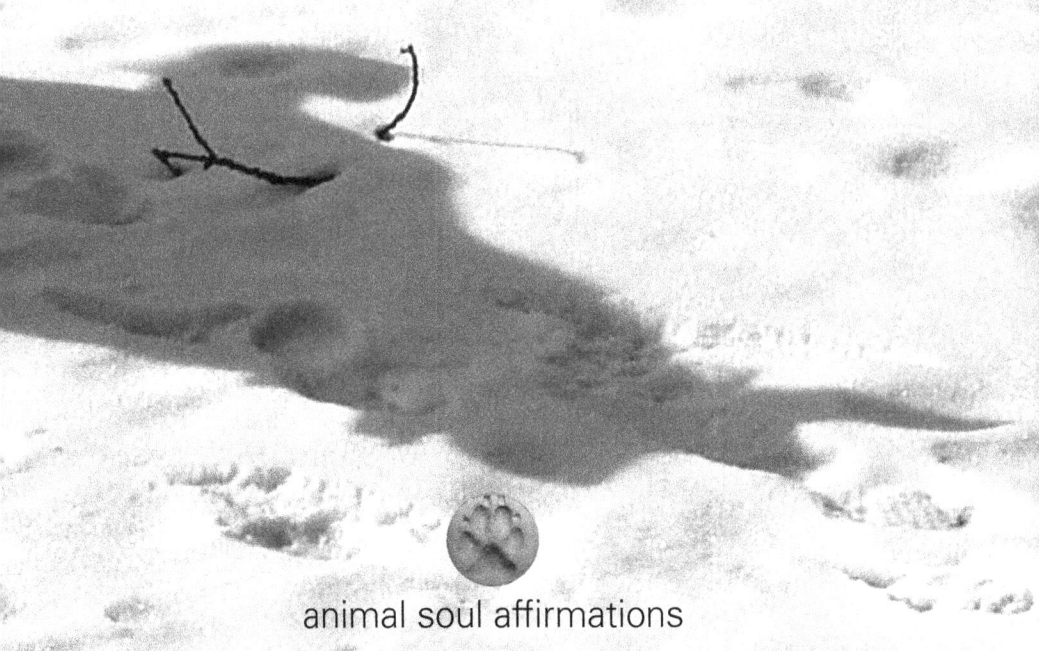

animal soul affirmations

© Copyright 2013 by Margo Bowblis

Printed and bound in the United States of America. All rights reserved. No part of this book may be reproduced in any form, or by any electronic or mechanical means, including information storage and retrieval systems, without permission in writing from the publisher, except by a reviewer, who may quote brief passages in a review.

Published by:
    animal soul affirmations
    27 Dogwood Trail • Kinnelon, NJ 07405
    Email: animalsoul2006@aol.com
    Visit us at:
    www.walkingwiththeshadowoflove.com

To purchase copies of this book,
contact the publisher above.

Printed in the United States of America

Produced by:
White Oak Editions, Seaman, OH 45679
cartaino@aol.com
Carol Cartaino, editor

animal soul affirmations

Dedication

Not all heroes wear uniforms and run into burning buildings. There are those among us who are extraordinary. They exist in all walks of life, all professions, and even in our personal connections. What is extraordinary about them is their capacity to empathize and love. These qualities are the driving force in their lives, and allow them to go above and beyond all normal expectations in caring for others—even when they are in intense personal, emotional, and/or physical pain.

This book is dedicated to Dr. Kara Seiford. No, that is not her real name. But she knows who she is, and when she reads this book, she will recognize her work. As long as I walk this earth, she will always be my hero.

Acknowledgements

Special thanks to:
- Carol Cartaino of White Oak Editions, who took a step into the unknown, and applied her abundant knowledge and expertise to this book for this lucky author! She took a chance on a dark horse—uh, dark dog—to make this book a reality for a totally unknown writer/artist.
- Demitrius of Infinity Photography in Pompton Plains, New Jersey, for generously sharing his artistry by allowing me the use of his beautiful photographs for this book and its publicity.
- "Dr. Kara Seiford," and all the vets at "Animals First" who generously donated their time, help, and compassion; and all of the other exceptionally kind, caring, good people there.
- And all the vets and techs everywhere who are kind, gentle, and loving to their patients, even though those patients cannot speak or complain when they are treated harshly or cruelly.
- Every person who loved The Zeakie Dog and helped my husband Bill and me with our dogs through this

difficult time, including but not limited to: (listed here alphabetically): Cathy, Donna, Laurie, and Linda.

- Every dog who loved The Zeakie Dog: Lakota, Ice, Molly, Cooper, Shy, and unnamed others.

- My girlfriends (listed here alphabetically): Cathy, Donna, Doreen, Jill, Laurie, Linda, Mary-Ellen, Sandy, and Suze—for dogsitting, bringing me lunch and company to keep me from feeling cut off when I had to stay home with my sick dog, and helping me keep my spirits up. When the chips are down, your girlfriends always have your back.

- To Bill for his technical expertise, work, support, and input on this book, and to (listed alphabetically) Doreen, Laurie, Len, Linda, Mary-Ellen, Sandy, and my son, Tom, for proofreading and other input.

- To Donna, for the help, care, kindness, and the knowledge she generously shared with me. For constantly answering my questions, contacting experts she knew for information, calling everywhere to help me find a cooling mattress despite her busy schedule, and always, always, always being there when I needed her.

- To my therapist, for his help and support with this book, grief support, and—most importantly—for not pronouncing me crazy!

- To Dr. Bob, for waging the battle on the nutritional and holistic front, and to Jaime, for her support, compassion, and kindness.

- To Cinder, Santana, Lakota, and The Zeakie Dog—for your unconditional, incredible, limitless love.

Table of Contents

The Time Has Come ....Introduction
A Therapy Dog Visit ....Chapter 1
A Dog Again ....Chapter 2
The First Visit ....Chapter 3
Training a Therapy Dog ....Chapter 4
The Zeakie Dog ....Chapter 5
Play Date ....Chapter 6
O.C.D. and the Turds of Meditation ....Chapter 7
Doggie Day Care? ....Chapter 8
The Loft Ladder ....Chapter 9
Raising The Zeakie Dog ....Chapter 10
A Disturbing Visit ....Chapter 11
The Invisible Spot ....Chapter 12
Normal, Sweet Normal ....Chapter 13
A Very Close Call ....Chapter 14
The Snake ....Chapter 15

The Aftermath	Chapter 16
Celebrating	Chapter 17
An Entertaining (and Strange) Party	Chapter 18
Another Visit	Chapter 19
The Beginning	Chapter 20
Our Foe Revealed	Chapter 21
To Fight or to Say Goodbye	Chapter 22
A Visit in My Room	Chapter 23
The Gift of Cancer	Chapter 24
Cooper and Ice	Chapter 25
The Fireplace	Chapter 26
The Last Winter	Chapter 27
The Last Spring	Chapter 28
The Last Summer	Chapter 29
A Dog in Macy's?	Chapter 30
MOPP	Chapter 31
Hurricane Irene and Other Disasters	Chapter 32
The Practical Joker	Chapter 33
The Last Autumn	Chapter 34
The World Conference: the Last Protocol	Chapter 35
The Beautiful Goodbye	Chapter 36
Jim's Story	Chapter 37
The Song and the Candle	Epilogue
About the Author	

Introduction:

The Time Has Come

This I know for certain: There will be believers and there will be non-believers, concerning the events that occurred when The Zeakie Dog passed from this existence to the next one…and certain occurrences that happened afterwards. I have lived as sane an existence as any of us. I had a long and successful career as an educator. And I was more in control of my emotions than a lot of people I have seen were, when they had to say goodbye to their beloved animals. I maintained that control, because I had to make decisions about him; and take the best care of him I possibly could, right till the end. I was calm and focused: what I saw, I saw.

Several of my friends were in attendance at the very end. One of them was standing behind me. She saw Zeakie staring at me through the window in the door at the vet's, and said that it appeared to her that his eyes were getting larger. I maintain that they weren't getting larger, they were getting CLOSER, so they appeared larger. As for me, I am changed forever by what happened on that day.

This book has two story lines that run concurrently. The first tells how each of the dogs arrived in my life, how they became therapy dogs, and some of their experiences as working therapy dogs. It follows their lives, documents a battle waged with cancer by a dedicated—even heroic—veterinary oncologist, and ends with an extraordinary, life-altering, spiritual happening that occurs as Zeak is dying.

The second story line, which is interspersed with the first one, all happens after November 13, 2011—the date Zeak passed on. While many dog stories end with the death of the dog, The Zeakie Dog's does not. These chapters are written in italics to distinguish them from the first story line. They record events that occurred, and—as of this writing—continue to occur; in which The Zeakie Dog makes his presence and his continued existence known. He does this because, above all else, this book is a love story.

Many people have experienced such occurrences, such as the neighbor I mention in this book. Numerous people have told me about their own experiences with afterlife contacts with their beloved animals and people, when I shared the things that happened to me. People are uncomfortable about coming forward on this subject, so they keep secrets about these events. But I believe it is time to stand up and be counted, because events like this will alter the perception humans have of animals. And the time for that has come, and is in fact, long overdue.

One of the most common afterlife contacts I hear about from people is, "I thought I saw my (dog, cat, loved person, etc.), out of the corner of my eye." There is a reason these sightings are always seen that way. Astronomers call it "averted gaze." It has to do with the structure of our eyes. At the center of our retinas are cells called "cones," whose function is to see color. They are at their highest concentration when you are looking directly ahead of you, because they are located near the center. At the outer edges of our retinas are the "rods." These cells see movement and faint light and are more sensitive and numerous than the cones. That is why a faint star will look brighter if not gazed at directly. And that is why a faint spirit will be seen "out of the corner of your eye," and then disappears when you look at it directly. Maybe people shouldn't be so quick to dismiss those sightings that disappear when they look directly at them.

If you still need convincing, I recommend reading *Animals and the Afterlife,* by Kim Sheridan, published by Hay House. This book contains many stories of animals who have made afterlife contact with their previous owners. The owners of these animals have included their names, occupations, and locations with their stories; and they come from all walks of life. There are so many such stories that the author is working on a sequel, because there were too many to include in one book. However, my experience is unique, to my knowledge: I have never come across anything like this in anything I have read or heard about.

If you have loved and lost a pet, and hungered for some kind of sign or contact from them, please do not feel that you are being forgotten if you have not received it. First of all, these occurrences are subtle. I am by nature very sensitive. I sometimes pick up on things that others might miss—not because I try to—it's just my nature. Sometimes it's not such a blessing! We are all wired differently, and I have no idea why I have been so fortunate as to have these affirmations from my dog. I believe it has much more to do with this very special dog, than it does with me. The reason I believe that is because my heart has been broken before, by loss of dogs and people I loved; but nothing like this ever happened.

The events in this book are as factual as my memory can make them. I have changed names and locations, and other specifics, to protect people's privacy. I have also avoided going into so much detail as to encumber the plot. My intention in writing this book is straightforward: I want to share this story, which happened to me, because it has expanded and enlightened my whole concept of animals and their spirituality—and I hope it will expand and enlighten yours.

I know what I saw. And never, in my wildest imagination, could I have concocted such an event, or the occurrences that followed. If you have ever endured the pain of deeply loving and losing an animal, then the events in this book will give you hope and comfort, as they have to me. If you have ever wondered if animals have souls, this book will shed a new light on that question. I only ask that you read this with an open mind and an open heart. If you do that, I believe the truth will ring out to you. And when it does, it will leave you questioning everything you have ever thought about animals before.

Margo Bowblis

*I directed Lakota's attention to the woman's face,
and then he went to work.*

CHAPTER 1

A Therapy Dog Visit: June 2007

The music funneled down the long hallway. The woman's angelic voice—with no accompaniment—was unexpected here. My therapy dog, a black Labrador Retriever named Lakota, and I had finished our rounds in the rehabilitation building at Pine Hill Senior Community. We were about to leave for home, when I heard the music and saw the young woman standing alone at the end of the hallway. I decided we could make one more stop, so we headed down the hall. The woman was a tall, attractive brunette and she smiled as we approached. I introduced myself, and asked if she would like to say hello to Lakota. She said she would love to, and knelt down and gave Lakota a gentle hug as he licked her face. It was obvious that she was very comfortable around dogs.

I commented on the lovely voice we were all listening to. She told me that she had hired the singer to sing her mother's favorite songs to her. Her mother was dying, and had been spiraling downward for some time. Now she had been removed from the wires, machines, and tubes that were no longer able to sustain life. The daughter then made a request: she asked me if we would be willing to visit a person who was dying. She said that her mother had always had dogs, and that black Labs were her favorites. I assured her that this was a part of the services that therapy dogs offered. A few minutes later the singer finished and left, and we entered the room. I braced myself, thinking this would be difficult. Instead, I was about to experience something surprising and deeply moving.

The old woman in the bed was silent and motionless. Her long, gray hair was neatly brushed, and fell down below her shoulders. She was lying on her back, and her mouth was wide open. A nurse's aide was with her. Everything was immaculate. This was a top-notch facility. When her daughter sat down beside her and took her hand, there was no response. The young woman told her mother that a handsome black Lab was here to visit her. I gave Lakota the "paws up" command, and he stood up on his hind legs and rested his head and the front half of his body on the bed, right by the old woman's face. Her daughter told the dying woman that she wanted her to feel how soft Lakota's fur was, and that she was going to put her hand on the dog's head for her. She did so. No response.

I directed Lakota's attention to the woman's face, and then he went to work. He licked her face, and as he did so, she started to smile. The smile turned to silent laughing. Tears were trickling down her daughter's face as she choked out the words, "She's laughing!" Then the nurse's aide lost it, and so did I, and all three of us were in tears. I had heard that animals seem to be able to negotiate the transition between this life and the next more easily than humans—that they seem to be able to reach the unreachable. But this was the first time I had witnessed it firsthand. The nurse's aide told me that she had seen therapy dogs around the building, but had never seen anything like this. She said that now she "got it."

After a few minutes, I gave Lakota the "off" command and he got down. I felt it was time for us to leave. As we started to go I put my hand on the daughter's shoulder. No words were necessary. I took one more look at the old woman, and noticed that she now appeared beautiful to me. Her features had not changed one bit. She was back to being totally unresponsive again. But she looked different now—some kind of transformation had taken place. She looked peaceful and radiant and I felt filled with energy, even though I had been very tired when I entered the room. I couldn't help but feel that this woman was someone very special. I realized that I was witnessing a loving, peaceful passing. This woman's daughter had been able to get past the usual pain and trauma of letting go of someone she loved deeply, and plan a loving passing for her mother. And our chance arrival had added one more loving, tender element to it. This was our first visit with a person who was passing right before our eyes. Rather than being sad and difficult, as I thought it would be, it had been mesmerizing.

If someone had told me a few years ago that I would be doing this, I would not have believed them. I had been too ill, and very allergic to dogs for twenty years. Because of this, I had not had a dog for all that time. Before that, dogs had always been a big part of my life. Growing up, our family had four dogs during the years I lived at home. When I was in my twenties and thirties I had owned, bred, trained, and shown Labradors. When I lost my last dog from that period of my life, my heart broke. I became seriously—dangerously—allergic to animals of all kinds. I wondered if I was protecting myself from ever going through that kind of pain again. I had a close connection to that dog. He was a magnificent black Lab named Santana, with a head that looked chiseled from stone. He was at my side all the time. No leash necessary; nothing would tempt him to bolt. He was a show dog and a competition obedience dog. When he died I thought no dog could ever fill my heart again. I thought there could never be a dog I had a connection to like that. I thought there could never be a dog I would find that extraordinary. I was wrong.

Puppy Lakota was adorable.

CHAPTER 2

A Dog Again: April 2004

It was over eight years ago that the desire for another dog began to grow within my heart. I just needed a little push. Our friend Brian was staying with us at the time, and he provided that nudge. He was staying with us so he could save up money to buy a house, and in return was making some much-needed repairs to our home. He also had the yearning to have a dog around, and said he would help me with the work involved in raising a puppy. It didn't take much for the two of us to convince my husband Bill that this would be a great addition to our little family. I had just retired from my job as an art teacher due to a chronic condition that made me unable to continue to expend the energy necessary to teach. I felt I could handle a dog, provided I had a fenced-in yard for days I was too weak to walk him. Despite pledges from both of the guys that they would help, because they would be away at their jobs all day, I knew most of the work—and the pleasure—of caring for the dog would be mine. I also knew that while life sometimes brought changes and human relationships sometimes ended, a dog was a lifetime commitment for me. For that reason, I wanted the dog's ownership papers to be in my name. They both agreed that would be fine.

I discussed it with my married son, Tom, and he thought it would be great to have a playmate for his six-month-old puppy, a red Doberman Pinscher named Shy. He did give me a word of caution, though. He reminded me that there would never be another Santana. He said that a dog like that came only once in a lifetime and that it wasn't fair to put expectations like that on a new puppy. I agreed with him and thanked him for the heads-up. Next, I headed for my allergist.

My allergist said that while I was still allergic to dogs, my allergy was less severe due to lifestyle changes I had made, and that I would become desensitized to a dog that I lived with. I wanted another black Lab. I looked around the internet, searching for what I wanted: a hybrid—half field dog and half bench dog. The breeding of Labradors had split since I had my dogs forty-something years ago. I didn't want a pure field dog—a Lab bred for retrieving birds for hunters—because it would be too hyper. I did not have the energy to meet the needs of a dog like that, and when dogs don't get enough exercise it means trouble. And I didn't want a pure bench dog—a Lab bred to be a show dog—because they were a little too sedentary and tended to gain weight, which put them at risk for diabetes. I finally found what I was seeking from a breeder of Labradors in New York State. I checked her out with Lab Rescue in that area. When they told me they wouldn't need to exist if all breeders were as ethical as she was, I knew that this was where I would get my puppy.

Since it had been so long since I had a dog and I wanted to be totally prepared, I called my friend Donna, who was a trainer and the head of a rescue group. Donna knew more about dogs than anyone I knew, short of a vet. It was her lifetime passion, and she generously shared her time and expertise with me. She took me shopping, and I bought everything needed to raise a puppy, and then some. At the time I thought no dog but a black Lab could fill the longing I had, and I wanted to raise a puppy from scratch, so I did not entertain the idea of rescuing. Down the road, I was to learn I was wrong about that, too.

With everything in place at home, I made an appointment with the breeder to go and look at the pups who were ready for new homes. We decided to meet in one of her outbuildings, since the barn had cats and that was still a serious allergy of mine. I asked her if I could meet all the male pups—I had decided I wanted a boy—and also Mom and Pop if that were possible. I also made arrangements to speak with her vet's office and get information on the pups' and the parents' hips, heart, and eyes, so as to avoid any serious congenital problems. And I had decided on a name: "Lakota." It was a Native American word for "friend." It was also the name of a tribe with a rich culture and history. I also wanted to honor my great-grandmother, a Native American from New York State who had thirteen children—one of them, my grandfather on my mother's side.

With all of our homework done, Bill and Brian and I headed up to New York State to "look" at puppies. None of us really thought we were going to just look. We all knew we would be bringing home a pup. We arrived right on time and pulled into the parking lot of the building the breeder had directed us to. Barely a minute later, a station wagon pulled in.

The woman who got out was so tiny, it was hard to imagine her running this huge breeding farm for dogs. But as soon as we made eye contact, I just knew she had unlimited energy and was a force of nature! I felt an instant bond with Melissa Weldon, even before she told me that she was also an artist. We chatted a while, and then she directed us to a different building that she would bring the puppies and parents to. We went inside and waited for her to get the puppies, and also their mom and dad. A few minutes later, four big, gorgeous, rollicking, black velvet puppies tumbled in the doorway!

The four brothers immediately started running around the room, sniffing everything and looking for mischief to get into. I sat on the floor and waited. I have always preferred to let my dogs choose me. I believe that they know whom they are supposed to be with. One at a time, and in no particular hurry, the four pups came to check me out. Once they sniffed me and I talked to them and petted them, they lost all interest and were too excited about exploring their new surroundings to bother with me…all except for the smallest male. He was adorable, and came back to visit me three more times. The last of those times I put the little red collar I had brought along on his neck, and told him that I trusted that he knew he belonged with me; so he was coming with me to his new home. I gave him his new name and picked him up. He snuggled comfortably in my arms and made no attempt to get away.

About this time, Melissa returned with Momma, "Misty," and Daddy, "Rhino." Momma was a very friendly, very tall field dog—too tall to be shown, because she exceeded the breed standard. Dad was shorter, but a huge one-hundred-twenty-pound bench dog, with an enormous head and a sunny disposition. I visited with Mom and Dad a while. They were both friendly, calm, and relaxed—even the field dog, to my surprise.

Melissa gave me several documents to sign, including one saying I agreed to always provide air conditioning for our new family member, because black Labs were heat intolerant. Another document asked me to pledge I would never tie Lakota out. Tying a dog out is a really bad idea. Many dogs accidently hang themselves when their collars and tie-out ropes/chains catch on things, and in addition they are helpless, sitting ducks for predators. Since I was in total agreement with these stipulations, I was more than happy to sign the documents. The third stated that if we were ever, for any reason, unable to keep Lakota, he was to go back to her—not to a shelter or rescue. That is what a responsible breeder does. They are responsible for every puppy they bring into the world from birth to death. I paid her and she gave us a kit of instructions, a shot card and vet examination certificate, and a fleece bone that she had rubbed on each of his brothers and sisters, as well as Mom and Dad.

At that moment, a sadness came over me. I wondered how animals feel when they are taken from everyone they know and love, never to see them again. They are so powerless in this world…so often unable to control or influence their fate. There are people who think animals have no emotions. They are so wrong.

The time had come for us to leave. I carried Lakota to our compact SUV, and rode in the back seat with the puppy on my lap. As we pulled out he started to cry. It was heartbreaking—he somehow knew he was leaving forever. I held him and promised him I would give him the best life I possibly could, and would love him forever. I told him I knew how sad he was to leave his family, but I was glad he was coming with me because I knew he would be loved and protected. After about fifteen minutes, he stopped crying and fell asleep on my lap.

I vowed to give him the softest landing possible, to make this transition the easiest I could for him. I knew how sad he must be, but Lakota was one of the lucky ones—starting his life going from a good breeder to a loving home.

I thought of all the dogs raised in puppy mills. Puppy mills are horrible mass-breeding facilities, where the breeding parent animals are in a cage for their entire lives. They are malnourished, never exercised, constantly bred, neglected, and often abused. Their offspring are thrown into crowded cages, also malnourished and never exercised. For that reason, they often have health issues. They are usually ripped from their mothers and siblings and sold to pet stores all over the country, where they are thrown into cages with no one to love and comfort them. How frightened and alone they must feel. Often they are ignored for weeks or even months. Dogs grieve losses of loved ones, just as humans do. I don't know how dogs survive this pain and are still able to love us like they do—completely, unselfishly, and unconditionally.

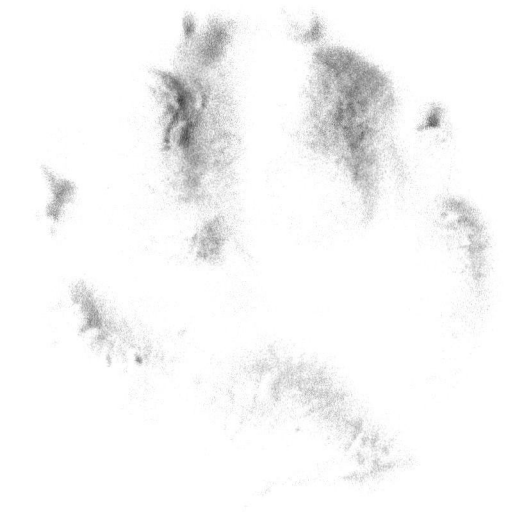

I couldn't move—couldn't breathe—could just be there with those eyes.

CHAPTER 3

The First Visit: After November 13, 2011

The first rays of light were filtering into my bedroom window and I was just coming into wakefulness, when it hit me like a punch in the face. It couldn't be true—this had to be a nightmare. A sick feeling in the pit of my stomach reminded me it was real. He was gone. The long battle was over, and we had lost—he had lost. My eyes were still closed, but tears were running down my face, when I saw the eyes. I saw them with my eyes closed, hovering in mid-air, two or three feet above me; looking down on me with such intensity that I didn't even feel the need to open my eyes. It didn't matter because this wasn't a dream. I was awake—awake and seeing with closed eyes, seeing the same incredibly intense eyes that had held me like a tractor beam in a sci-fi movie the day before, in Zeakie's final minutes. I couldn't move, couldn't breathe...could just be there with those eyes. Then, as it had before, a bolt of love hit me—struck me in the heart—one so strong that if it were any more intense it would have been painful, or paralyzed me. Silence. He was gone.

I had dozens of toys for Lakota. My formerly neat-as-a-pin house was cluttered with dog possessions all the time. He loved his toys and never touched even one thing of ours.

CHAPTER 4

Training a Therapy Dog: April 2004

The ride home was without incident. We stopped once, and let Lakota relieve himself. A couple of hours later we pulled into our driveway. Our home was a small, frame house in a beautiful lake community of lovely little homes, which had private hiking trails and bordered on many miles of watershed and preserved land. It was a great place for a dog, and there were a lot of them in our community. We even had an unofficial dog beach, where members could bring their dogs to swim and frolic in the cool water to beat the heat.

When I had my last dogs, nobody had crates. "Crate" is a politically correct term for "cage." Donna had suggested I buy one to keep the puppy safe at night and when I went out. I knew puppies could get into serious danger doing things like chewing electrical cords, so I went along with it. She also said that if a dog ever needed a stay at the vet, they would be less stressed if they were used to a crate. All of these reasons were very sound, but I need to interject here that I believe crates have not been a generally wonderful thing for dogs. New puppies need to empty their tiny bladders every half hour. Dogs are den animals but they are also pack animals. Far too many people stick a dog in a crate, go to work for eight hours, and if it's a puppy, let it soil its crate and then they have to live in it all day. This is deeply humiliating for a dog. And being in a crate all day is like being in jail for a crime you never committed. Dogs left alone all day get very lonely. Good solutions are to have two dogs and a dog walker, who will come mid-day and give your dogs some exercise and a nice outing. Many behavior problems arise from too little exercise, loneliness, and boredom.

Donna told me to make Lakota's crate an appealing place by having a nice, soft, cushion and a blanket in it, a few toys he could play with only in there, making them special, and feeding him in his crate. She also told me to leave the door open and hide treats in it. I followed her directions until it was time for bed. I knew the crate should be closed at night to keep the puppy safe, but it was too big to fit in our tiny bedroom. I was not going to let a lonely little puppy away from his family for the first time cry all night alone in a cage. So I got out a sleeping bag and pillow and set up right next to Lakota on the floor to spend the night. Bill and Brian decided to camp with us, so we all camped on the living room floor for the night. Lakota started to cry when I closed the door of his crate, so I stuck my fingers in through the bars and touched him, and he stopped immediately. I left my hand like that and we all had a peaceful night's sleep.

As soon as I opened my eyes the next morning, Lakota came alive—jumping up and down and prancing inside his jail…uh…crate. He was so adorable and excited. I opened his door and picked him up and took him outside right away. We just made it, and as he peed I told him what a good boy he was over and over. I gave him breakfast: a kibble that the breeder had sent me home with, and he gobbled it up. Unfortunately, that kibble was not available in our area, so I would have to gradually change him over to one I could buy locally. I had several recommendations from Donna, but Lakota would not eat any of them. It took a lot of samples and failures, and what I finally got him to eat, he would only eat from my hand. I suspect this was due to his grief over the loss of his family. After a few weeks of hand-feeding, he finally got into a normal eating pattern.

Lakota was so smart and eager to please that housebreaking was accomplished in three days... I stayed home with him and took him out every half hour or so and praised him when he "went" outside. When he had an accident I said "no," picked him up and brought him outside, and to indicate that he should go, used the expression "pit stop." Then, I told him what a good boy he was every time he went.

Lakota was a joy to have around, but at this stage I had little time for anything else and was exhausted by the end of each day. I knew that would get better as he got older, could hold it longer, and as he acclimated to me being gone some of the time. To accomplish the latter, I started leaving him in his crate for just a minute at first, then closing the door and going out to the mailbox, and gradually increasing the amount of time I left him. This worked well, but Lakota never liked the crate. He obeyed and went in and scarfed down the treats I left in it. But he wasn't buying it at all.

I had dozens of toys for him. My formerly neat-as-a-pin house was cluttered with dog toys all the time. He loved his toys and never touched even one thing of ours. So one day when he was four months old and he gave me the "please don't make me go in there" look when I was going out, I decided he was ready to have the run of the house. I told him I would be back soon and left the crate door open. When I came back, all was well. After that, he never went into the crate unless I asked him to, and then he would come right back out. Since it was taking up way too much room in our little living room, I folded it and put it away. Once a year I get it out, put goodies in there, and let him stay a few minutes to remind him it's OK.

We called a local fencing company and had a large area—the whole back yard—fenced in with a chain link fence six feet high. We wanted this so Lakota could go out on his own when I was home, and also to protect him from bears, coyotes, and other predators that are plentiful in our area. Despite being told that this fence was for a dog yard, however, the fencing company made some major mistakes. The first one was to leave sharp bolts on the inside without capping them. One day Lakota was chasing a ball around and ran into one of these bolts. It missed his eye by a quarter of an inch and tore an inch-long gash in his face. I took him to our vet and he refrained from stitching it, but said it might leave a scar. It didn't, but this was just the beginning of the injuries caused by this fence.

I started training him to walk on a leash, and to obey the commands sit, down, and stay. He was a quick study and soon had all of that down nicely. He had begun to have bursts of wildness, however, where he would act like a bucking bronco at the end of a leash, jump on me with all his might, and tear around the yard so fast he would occasionally run into me. I had never experienced this with my other Labs. I was actually sustaining bruises from this behavior until one day I had it out with him: I literally had to wrestle him to the ground and lay him down on his side with a firm "no." This was no easy feat, and did me in for the rest of the day. I was waiting to neuter him till he was close to a year old. I was reluctant to do what many people do and neuter young, because I had read there are some studies showing puppy neutering increases cancer risk and it's better to wait till they are one year old. I also decided to enroll him in a class so he would get used to behaving around other dogs.

Since I was too tired at night to do dog training and take Donna's class in dog obedience, I looked for a daytime class.

The only one I could find was one with a trainer who worked full time at a facility that trained seeing-eye dogs. He had a reputation for being really tough with very high standards. So Lakota and I enrolled in doggy boot camp. Most of the training was the same as it was with my last dogs, with one notable exception: the "leave-it" command. This new command was sheer brilliance. It covered everything from the dog helping himself to hors d'oeuvres from the coffee table, to running out of the bedroom with my underwear in his mouth in front of guests, to eating goose poop by the lake.

After the eight-week class, Lakota and the other nine dogs in the class took the AKC Canine Good Citizen Test. As noted earlier our trainer was very exacting; out of the ten dogs, only two passed. Lakota was one of them and I was very proud of him. He was just right: not too submissive, thus other dogs didn't pick on him, but very generous—he would share his toys and showed no sign of jealousy when I gave affection to other dogs he was playing with. Some of my neighbors and I had a dog group. We took group walks together, and had play dates and birthday parties for our dogs.

Donna and I went out to lunch to celebrate, and she asked me if I knew about the work that therapy dogs were doing. I didn't, and she filled me in. She had two therapy dogs who visited hospitals, nursing homes, schools, and even did home visits for bedridden or housebound people living with caretakers. She also had a therapy dog with advanced training who was a disaster assistance dog. He had comforted families and first responders at the World Trade Center in the days following the attack. People who were so traumatized they couldn't talk just hugged her dog and petted him and cried and found some comfort that they couldn't find in another human being. She told me that she thought Lakota had the right stuff to become a therapy dog, so we set out to desensitize him to wheelchairs, walkers, hospital equipment, and noisy machinery. He was a rock. He had calmed down so much he was unshakable.

I felt very prepared and confident in my boy when the time came to take the test for therapy dog certification. We walked into a local firehouse to find about thirty dogs there to be tested. The only part of the test that worried me was a child sitting in a wheelchair with a cheeseburger on his lap. Cheeseburgers were Lakota's favorite thing on earth. We had to walk by the "distraction" with a slack leash and could only use our voice and the "leave-it" command to control our dogs. I gave the command with the intensity in my voice of a general leading a charge to save his country, just to be sure Lakota knew this was serious. He resisted the temptation and became a certified therapy dog.

We started visiting local facilities and I discovered a deep sense of satisfaction in the joy we were able to give the people we visited. Time after time people would tell me that our visit "made their whole day." I particularly enjoyed visiting seniors who had pets their whole lives and now were in assisted living or nursing homes with no animals, and deeply missed them. One man told me tearfully that when he had to move into assisted living, his dog was euthanized because it was old and no one wanted it. He told me he feared he would never get to be with a dog again, and what a nice surprise it was to have dogs visiting him here.

Shy—my son's young red Doberman Pinscher.

CHAPTER 5

The Zeakie Dog: June 2006

It was the summer of Lakota's second year. We were enjoying walks around the lake and group dog swims, with the dogs swimming as fast as they could to retrieve balls and sticks that we threw in the lake. Lakota saw his dog friends every day, and handling the work, exercise, and cost of one dog was enough of a challenge, so I had no intention of having a second one. Our friend Brian had moved out and had bought a cabin in a lake community about forty minutes north of where we lived. My son, daughter-in-law, and grandson lived not far from where Brian lived, so they saw each other frequently. One night, Tom called to tell me that Brian had brought his new puppy over to visit them. He said that Brian had done everything knowledgeable dog people tell us not to do. He went into a pet store, saw a puppy, and bought it because he just couldn't leave it there. (Later on, I was to learn from Donna that this particular pet shop had numerous outbreaks of bordatella—the dog version of a cold—and even the deadly parvovirus.) The puppy had been languishing in a cage in the store for so long that it was "On Sale."

I told my son that places like this were where puppies from puppy mills were sold. I wondered how Brian was going to care for a puppy when he worked all day and had a long commute. Tom said that Brian's girlfriend, who had moved in with him, would take care of it during the day while he was at work. He told me that despite the circumstances of its arrival, there was "something about" this puppy—he couldn't explain it any more than that. He encouraged me to come and see it because it had "really striking" markings. So we headed north to meet the new puppy. Never could I have imagined that the little fellow I was about to meet was going to rock my whole world, shake me to my core, and change me and who I was, and what I cared about...forever.

We arrived at my son and daughter-in-law's house and entered. The puppy was playing with Shy, their two-and-a-half-year-old red Doberman Pinscher. As soon as we walked in, the two dogs came to greet us. The puppy was small and black, with enormous ears that looked like a full-grown German Shepherd's. He had perfectly symmetrical white speckled "boots" on his front legs, perfectly symmetrical white feet on his back legs, and on his chest was a perfectly centered pure white cross; which in certain positions turned into an arrow, pointing down. The markings were so precise that they looked like they were painted on. Brian told me that the pup was half Border Collie and half German Shepherd, two of the most intelligent breeds. He said that the puppy was smart—so smart that it was almost scary.

The puppy and Lakota bonded instantly. Even the pup's sharp teeth, nipping at Lakota's back legs in an attempt to "herd" him, couldn't discourage Lakota from wanting to be with this pup. I sat on the couch, and then the puppy, who Brian had named "Zeak," came to check me out.

We all have heard of love at first sight. They make movies about it, write poetry describing it, and sing songs of glory about it. All I know is that when my eyes met the puppy's, I felt my heart jump, and a wave of emotions washed over me. And it was obvious that the feeling was mutual. Yes, puppies are adorable and I had been around my share of them, but I had never felt anything like this upon meeting a new pup.

The small dog with the giant ears and I had quite a thing for each other.

When it was time for us to leave, the pup started crying as I approached the door. As I walked out the door, the cries turned to yelps, and the yelps turned into bone-rattling, gut-wrenching screams. It was upsetting to everyone. But the simple truth was: the puppy knew whom he belonged with…who the person was that he came into this world to spend his life with. And that person was not his owner. It was me. And as I pulled out of the driveway, I could still hear his screams.

The small dog with the giant ears and I had quite a thing for each other.

CHAPTER 6

Play Date: After November 13, 2011

I lie in bed, hoping and praying that his eyes will come back to me—that he will come back to me. He doesn't. If Lakota didn't need to go out, I'm not sure I could ever get out of bed again. I go through the usual morning routine. His brother gone, Lakota won't eat his breakfast. I can't eat mine. Elaine calls to tell me her dog Cooper threw up his breakfast. She suggests we get the dogs together for a play date, thinking it might help them through this. She also invites our friend Erin and her adopted pup, Tundra.

Lakota and I are the last to get there. As we enter the room, Tundra and Lakota get into some very rough dog play—that is, until Lakota carefully maneuvers around and...sits on Tundra's head. Suddenly, it's like the air has been sucked out of the room. Lakota is a mellow, middle-of-the-pack dog. He has never, ever in his life, done anything like that. Tundra is a very dominant young dog—the "heir apparent" new leader of the dog pack. Did we all just see that? Lakota would not do that. Only The Zeakie Dog would do that to Tundra, and in fact did—several times. I wondered: is Zeak acting through Lakota to let us know he is here? To let us know he still is? To let us know he is OK?

We hiked to the dog beach, and I threw some sticks out into the water for Lakota to retrieve. In this picture, Lakota takes the high road and ignores the Canada Geese—training over DNA!

CHAPTER 7

O.C.D. and the Turds of Meditation: October 2006

Lakota was maturing into an almost adult dog—he was between two and three years old—and had survived his fence injury without a scar on his beautiful face. After that incident, Bill had glued caps on all of the sharp bolts facing in on the fence, and we thought that our fence problems were over.

My morning routine consisted of getting the house straightened up, breakfast for us and Lakota, and meditating for fifteen minutes. Next, I would go out into the dog yard to pick up the morning poop. Lakota always came with me on this mission, and he watched with great interest as I bagged the stuff and carried it around front to the poop can. Sometimes I would throw a ball for Lakota to chase a few times, too.

One morning I was deep into my meditation when Lakota, who would usually lie quietly by my side when I was doing this, came flying in the dog door from outside. He quickly settled down by my side, and I never opened my eyes—I just kept focused on my breathing. At least, that is, until my breathing smelled…poop!

Pulled out of my peaceful reverie by the offending odor, I looked down, and to my horror saw two large, fragrant turds on the wall-to-wall carpeting right by my feet! Lakota was looking up at me like he did when he had done something wonderful during training, and expected a treat. He had gone out into the yard and brought me this gift. In a truly horrified voice I said, "No!" I got a bag, picked up the two still-warm poops and took them outside. From my demeanor, poor Lakota was quickly realized that his "gift" had not been appreciated. I set about steaming the rug, grumbling to myself all the while.

As I pushed the heavy steamer around I began to calm down a little, and looked at this incident from my dog's point of view: "Every morning Mommy comes out into the yard and picks up my poop. She must really like this stuff. I bet she'd really like it a lot if I brought her some." This was simple logic from my eager-to-please Lab. Labs love to help more than anything. Fortunately, my reaction had been enough to convince Lakota that perhaps this wasn't such a great idea after all. Just to be sure, I always closed the dog door before I meditated after that.

Unless it was pouring out, after I meditated, I would strap on my hiking pack, leash up Lakota, and head down to the trail at the end of our street. Most mornings we would meet up with some of our dog-friends: both dogs and their owners, and start our morning trek. We would all unleash the dogs as we walked the trails around the lake and the dogs would tear around the woods chasing each other, jumping over fallen trees and running so hard we could actually feel the ground under our feet shake! It was a beautiful sight, seeing them in their element. They could run through all the underbrush and trees at full speed, and react so fast that they could avoid collisions. They would really get overheated during these sessions, and when that happened we would stop at the unofficial dog beach—a spot where the trail came close to the lake and there was a strip of dirt with enough room to stand on. The dogs would fly into the lake, enjoying the cooling effect of the water.

One morning, none of our friends could join us. I made sure I threw the ball a bunch of times in the dog yard before we left to give Lakota some hard running exercise, because without the other dogs he would not be running around in the woods. He would just walk by my side. We hiked to the dog beach and I threw some sticks out into the water for Lakota to retrieve. When he came out, I noticed him licking his leg, down near the ankle. I lifted it to examine it and saw a deep cut that had sliced his dew claw pad—the highest pad a dog has on his foot—almost completely in half. I took out my first aid kit and bandaged it. I wondered if there was broken glass in the lake. What I didn't know was that my dog's injury had happened an hour ago in my own yard, and that Lakota was once again a victim of our own fence.

I called my vet's office and let them know we were coming in with an injury. When we got there, they took us right away. Dr. Weaver said that he could repair the injury with a local anesthetic and staples. A short time later, Lakota and a vet tech emerged from the operating room. The whole lower half of Lakota's leg was bandaged, and—much to his horror—he had a cone on his head! For those of you not familiar with this, a cone or Elizabethan collar is a large, stiff, plastic collar that extends way beyond the animal's head. It is used to prevent animals from ripping out their stitches/staples, or licking their wounds to the point of injury. The vet tech told me to keep it on him, because he was going to want to get at the wound and lick it. Neither she nor I had any idea what we were in for, and how profoundly true that statement was going to turn out to be.

Over the next seven days, I made no less than seven trips to the vet. Each day, Lakota managed to get his cone off, and obsessively ripped out his staples, stitches, and glue—in that order. Three different types of cones fell to his assault. I was very embarrassed, but no cone could stop Lakota from licking/chewing on his wound.

I had been staying with Lakota to watch him all I could, but I had to go up the ladder to my desk in the loft of our home to pay some bills. It was around seven p.m. on a crisp fall night, and Lakota was on my bed napping peacefully in his cone. I was upstairs about twenty minutes or so. When I came downstairs I went into the bedroom to check on Lakota. What I saw was puzzling: the cone was still on him, but the three and a half feet of veterinary wrap bandage—white with blue paw prints—was gone. I called Bill downstairs and explained the seriousness of the situation. We had to find the vet-wrap because if we couldn't find it, it would mean that the dog had eaten it.

Lakota had a mild form of O.C.D. (obsessive-compulsive disorder: the gene for this was discovered in dogs a few years ago, and it explains why dogs do things like this) and was an obsessive licker. If he had an itch or a bug bite, he would lick himself raw if I didn't stop him. What if he somehow reached around the cone and grabbed the vet-wrap and started licking and swallowing? I didn't want to think about the consequences: gastric surgery was thousands of dollars, painful, and risky. After searching the whole house, we headed out to the dog yard with flashlights. We lived in the woods. The leaves in the dog yard were five inches deep. We started at one end and sifted through the leaves, until we had covered the whole yard. I knew that Labrador Retrievers were known for eating things they shouldn't.

I called Dr. Weaver's office AGAIN. Being long past embarrassment, I explained what had happened. The receptionist asked me to hold on. She came back and told me the vet said one of four things would happen. One: the bandage would digest. Two: the dog would throw it up, hopefully not choking on the three-and-a-half-foot-long bandage. Three: the dog would pass the bandage through its digestive system and, well, you get the picture. Or four: it would cause an obstruction in his bowel and he would need major surgery.

This was the first time dog ownership was to bring me to my knees—it would not be the last. I got down on my knees, leaning on the side of my bed where Lakota was resting peacefully, and prayed to God for option one or option three. I prayed, pleaded, and begged. I couldn't sleep all night worrying about my dog. He, however, snored blissfully all night long.

On the second morning after the disappearance of the vet-wrap, Lakota went out the dog door after breakfast. About twenty minutes later he came back in, in a state I'd never seen him in before. I would describe it as extreme mortification. His ears were hanging so low they had become part of his neck. His tail hung lifeless. His head was down so low it was almost touching the kitchen floor. He would not look at me. Deep shame.

Hope surged in my heart. I walked to the back of the dog and carefully, ever so gently, lifted up the hanging tail. About an inch of vet-wrap was sticking out of the dog's rear! I was thrilled to see it until I realized that it was stuck there. It was not coming out on its own, and that was why Lakota was mortified. I called Donna's cell phone number, and (thank you, Lord!) she answered. She told me that I had to pull it out, S-L-O-W-L-Y. She said that if I did it too quickly I could cause serious injury. She ended with: "You might want to put on vinyl gloves."

Dog ownership is not for the squeamish. I was so afraid of the repercussions of this situation that, without hesitation, I grabbed gloves and took Lakota outside. I maneuvered him into a corner in the fence, told him to "stay," and started

S-L-O-W-L-Y pulling. It seemed like the vet-wrap had grown to about twenty feet long, but when all was said and done, it all came out—three and a half feet of white vet-wrap, but no blue paw prints. They had been digested. I called Dr. Weaver's office and told them that we had had a blessed event. The woman at the desk snickered and then she said, "All's well that ends well!" I hung up, hoping I would not have to see her or anyone there for a long time. Then I got on my knees again and said a heartfelt "Thank You."

I also took Donna out to lunch and made a contribution to her rescue. Considering all the help she had been giving me, I decided if I won the lottery, I should at least buy her a new car!

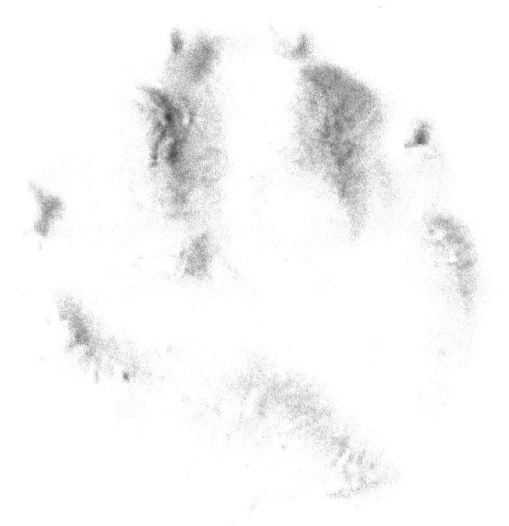

...and as we bonded with the puppy more and more, I decided we would find a way to afford another dog.

CHAPTER 8

Doggie Day Care? November 2006

Around the time that Lakota was recovering from his paw-pad injury, we got a call from Brian. We had seen him and his puppy several times since that first meeting, and always the scene was the same when we left. Whether we left them at my son's house, or at Brian's house, did not matter: the puppy would cry and yelp and scream as we left. If Brian brought him to our house for a visit, the puppy would do the same thing, as he carried him out the door. So it seemed that fate was siding with the puppy, when Brian told me that he was in a bind, and was hoping I could help him. He and his girlfriend had split up, and the puppy was too young to stay home alone for as long a day as Brian's job plus commute added up to. He was wondering if he could drop the puppy off on the way to work, let him hang out with Lakota, and pick him up on the way home. Since Lakota and I were crazy about Zeak, I quickly answered in the affirmative.

So every morning Brian would drop off the puppy, who would give us all a very enthusiastic greeting. And every evening, Brian would carry the loudly protesting puppy out to his truck for the ride home. We were beginning to feel the same way the puppy did. We all hated when the time came for him to go home. On weekends, we missed Zeak. Lakota was obviously looking for him at the window every time a car went by. And while none of us missed the wounds we were sustaining from the sharp puppy teeth, we all missed the puppy.

When the puppy was several months of age, Brian's vet recommended neutering Zeakie, as we had all started calling him. Brian was a little nervous about post-surgical care, so he asked me if I would mind coming up and staying over, to be there the first night after Zeakie's operation, in case anything were to go wrong. Since this was Brian's first dog, I was happy to accommodate him, as long as Lakota could come. Bill was OK with anything as long as he had something to eat for dinner. So Brian dropped Zeakie off at the vet's on the way to work, and the vet was to call me when Zeakie was able to be picked up, and Lakota and I would pick him up and head to Brian's.

Lakota had been quite sick from the anesthesia after he was neutered, but when I picked up Zeakie, he was fine. I drove to Brian's and let myself and the two dogs in with the key he had given me, and waited for him to get home from work. As soon as the puppy was up to it, I took the two dogs out, and went for a short walk. I had gotten a dog coupler—a strap connecting the two dogs that in turn connected to my leash, like a "Y." It made walking two dogs simultaneously much easier, as it didn't tangle. Brian arrived with a pizza an hour or two later. We ate and watched some TV and kept a close eye on the puppy. Lakota seemed to understand the whole of what was happening, and was very gentle with his little pal.

Since Brian's cabin had only one bedroom, he had made it up for Lakota and me, and he was going to sleep on the couch. Up until now, Zeakie liked to sleep in his crate—the door was always open. When it came time to retire, Lakota and I headed for the bedroom. I climbed into bed in my sweats, so that in case I had to do any kind of dog care, I could get out of bed in a hurry. Lakota jumped up on the bed and curled up next to me, as he usually did.

A few minutes later, I heard the puppy crying. I reached over and turned the light on, to find Zeakie trying to climb up on the bed. I got up and helped him up on the bed. When

I got back in and turned the lights off, he climbed onto me and snuggled his head into the left side of my neck as I lay on my back. Within seconds, he was asleep. I wrapped my arms around the soft, furry little body (minus a couple of parts), and fell asleep. I have always been a restless, poor sleeper. But when I awakened the next morning, Zeakie and I had not moved. I helped him off the bed, let the two dogs out, fed them, and prepared to head for home with both of them. We continued with this arrangement of Zeak staying with me during the day, and Brian picking him up and dropping him off again the next morning.

After a few months of this, Brian had another life-changing event: he lost his job. A victim of the economic downturn, he was laid off, and now he was thinking of training for a new job as a long-haul truck driver. There was just one thing complicating his decision: the puppy. So, Brian came to talk with us about his situation. He explained his employment plans, and then asked me a question: Since Zeak had wanted to be with me from day one, would I be receptive to adopting him? He said that he would want to be able to visit the puppy when he was in town, and asked how we felt about that.

Actually, this was no surprise to me. I worried about handling two big dogs and providing them with everything they needed—financially, exercise-wise, and training-wise. But I had seen this coming for a while, and as we bonded with the puppy more and more, I had decided we would find a way. Bill was also delighted. My only concern was I didn't want Brian to change his mind if circumstances changed. So I insisted on paying him what he had paid for the puppy, and having him sign him over to me in a notarized document. I told him he could visit Zeak whenever he liked. And so, The Zeakie Dog became mine, and—as surely as if he also had a notarized document—I became his.

And so, The Zeakie Dog became mine.

CHAPTER 9

The Loft Ladder: After November 13, 2011

It was around 1:30 in the afternoon of the day after Zeakie's passing. I had come back from Elaine and Allie's house still in a state of shock, with a depressed Lakota in tow. I decided to go up to the loft to see if I could do some mindless paper sorting. My eyes and face burned from crying, and I was physically sick from grief. I was desperate to get away from it for even a few minutes.

As I approached the ladder I began to feel guilty about leaving Lakota, who was also suffering. That is until I looked down, and to my left, to a bizarre sight: Lakota was smiling the biggest possible smile and, with a grand, sweeping motion, using his not-quite-long-enough-to-pull-it-off nose to gesture up the stairs. This was Lakota, who hated me going up there—Lakota, who had howled like a wolf when I went up there, doing what The Zeakie Dog had done almost every time I went up there!

This was the third time today that things had happened that I could not help but believe were some kind of communication from Zeak—attempting to tell me that he was here, with us, and was OK, and was letting us know that. I dropped to the floor and hugged Lakota and then just lay there, trying to grasp everything that was happening.

Puppy Zeak sneaks a taste of the dog cake while Lakota pretends not to see.

CHAPTER 10

Raising The Zeakie Dog

The Zeakie pup was not in any way the handful that Lakota was...for me. He took all his puppy mischief and brattiness out on Lakota. Lakota took it all with great patience and generosity, and occasional yelps and screams as the puppy's herding instinct prompted him to use his razor-sharp puppy teeth on his adopted older brother's hind legs. I would intervene in these cases, and when I gave the puppy a firm "No!," Lakota would smile at me just like a human. I was amazed at Lakota's patience and love for the puppy. Zeakie could take anything from Lakota's mouth: rawhide chews, toys, rawhide flip chips—virtually anything he wanted, Lakota would give him. He showed no jealousy toward the pup at all. He was totally willing to share everything he had with Zeakie—even me. There was only one thing Lakota held onto, and it was as if they had agreed to it: the spot right next to me in bed. Other than that night after he was neutered, when he slept cuddled in my neck, Zeak never tried to take that spot. Even if he got into bed first, he would always leave room for Lakota there, and lie down closer to my feet.

It didn't take long for me to realize how intelligent the puppy was. Lakota was smart. My first Labs, Cinder and Santana, were smart. But Zeakie wasn't dog smart—he was *human* smart! I had never had a dog express himself so much, vocally. I don't mean barking. I mean other sounds. At first we found his sounds funny. That is, until we realized that they had consistency. By that I mean that each sound had the same meaning every time he made it. That's when we real-

43

ized that the puppy was actually trying to communicate with us through sounds—a kind of language! We called it "Zeakinese." If his ball rolled under the couch and he wanted it, he always made the same sound. If he was hungry, he made a deep, grunting noise. If he wanted to go for his walk and I wasn't moving fast enough, he made the same impatient whining noise a small child might make. He was even very vocal with the other dogs, and all of us in our group marveled at the unusually diverse sounds that came out of that dog's mouth.

Zeakie was also incredibly affectionate. He was so full of love, he just couldn't contain himself. This resulted in something we called "The Zeakie Dance." When I got up in the morning, he was so happy that he would prance with his front legs, while his big back end swung in an almost one-hundred-eighty-degree arc, from side to side. And his huge tail brushed anything in its path off the coffee table, end tables, window sills, or anything within reach. If I went out, he danced when I came home. If anybody he especially liked came to our door, they would get a Zeakie Dance. Lots of dogs move around when they get excited—it was a question of degree. This dog looked like he was doing the rumba! And the kisses: he would give me a dozen or so fast kisses—we called them rapid-fire kisses—that were so gentle they felt like they were from a tiny dog. He also gave gifts: Every morning he brought me a present—one of his toys. He wasn't looking to play—when he wanted that he would drop the toy in front of me. It was a gift of love, and he would put it on my lap and then kiss me. He gave gifts to all the people he loved the most. And the gifts he gave the most were his favorite toys.

As he grew and interacted with more dogs, it also became apparent that he was a true alpha dog. He was the leader of his pack. He was never mean—he never hurt another dog. They just all gave him first choice of what he wanted. It was like they looked up to him. Even dogs older than he was just followed him…including Lakota.

When Brian bought Zeak, the pet store had told him that the puppy would be a medium-sized dog. They told him Zeak was half Border Collie and half German Shepherd. There was just one little detail they were omitting: Zeakie's left rear leg had a perfectly formed double dewclaw. It was not a deformed mistake. It was perfect, and it just so happens that there are only a few breeds that bear that distinction. One of them is the Great Pyrenees, a giant breed of herding dog, and the double dewclaw is actually in the breed's standard. The Zeakie pup grew and grew. He grew way past being a medium-sized dog. Soon it became apparent that he was going to be bigger than Lakota. How much bigger was something I frequently wondered.

I decided to take Zeakie to obedience class. I started him in advanced obedience, because he already did everything in beginning obedience. He was so good it was embarrassing. The other dog owners in the class asked me what I was doing to get him to work so perfectly. I told them I worked with him five minutes a day. It was kind of like a really skinny model telling people she never diets, and can eat everything she wants, and never gain weight. Some of the people in the class were really struggling with very unruly dogs and I could tell they wanted to choke me!

Zeak always knew exactly what I wanted him to do, wanted to please me, and did it. It became easier and easier and I began to realize that there was some kind of inner communication going on between us. He was so much like me. We were both very sensitive and anxious. But Zeak's anxiety was calmed by the fact that he had total and complete trust in me. And he never let his anxiety stop him; he was so brave. He loved class and he loved training, so I decided that he also would be a therapy dog. He was a little more nervous around the wheelchairs and walkers than Lakota, but when he realized I wanted him to do it, he did it and got over his nerves.

When the time came for Zeak to take his test to be a therapy dog, he was the biggest dog in his class. As he lay waiting to be called up, a little, white, female toy poodle—who was waiting to take the test next to us—decided to get a better view of the proceedings. She climbed up on The Zeakie Dog's back, and perched there. Zeak didn't seem to mind one bit. He just peacefully stayed there himself, while people smiled at the sweet picture these two dogs, who were strangers up till now, made. Then he took the test, smiling for some of it. He loved to work. He passed his test with flying colors and became my second therapy dog. Now all I needed was the energy to work two dogs! Fortunately, there were no minimum requirements for therapy dogs, so I could do as much as I was able, and had no pressure on me.

I took my dogs to several different local facilities. As I worked the two dogs, the differences between them became apparent. Lakota was very attentive to me when we worked. He waited for me to direct his every move. Zeakie was different: He gravitated towards certain people. He knew exactly who needed him and what they needed. I mostly let him direct the visits because he knew what he was doing.

On one visit to a nursing home about a half-hour away, a nurse's aide took us around. We got to a particular room and she told me that it was an unusual situation. The room was occupied by a mother and her daughter. Since we had been trained to respect privacy, I asked no questions. We went in and Zeak quickly greeted the mother, but it was obvious that it was the daughter he was really interested in.

Because he was so large, he didn't need to do "paws up" to reach someone. His head was a little taller than hospital bed height. The young woman was lying in the bed on her side. Zeakie went over and gave her a gentle little kiss. The woman, who appeared to be in her thirties or forties, was childlike, and squealed with delight. She then asked the aide and me if Zeakie could get in bed with her.

The aide asked if he would do that, and if he would be careful. I had total faith in Zeakie's ability to do both. I asked the aide if she would please get a clean sheet to lay down next to the patient, to protect both patient and dog from any dirt or bacteria, as we had been trained to do. When the aide put the sheet down, I gave Zeakie the "Up" command. Instead of jumping up as most dogs would, he first—in slow motion—put his front end up on the bed. Then, ever so slowly, he lifted his rear half up onto the bed, one leg at a time. Then he gently lay down with such care and concern that it was obvious Zeakie knew the woman in the bed was very fragile. He snuggled up against her and she draped her arm over him. Then she asked, "Can he stay all day?" I told her that we couldn't do that because we had so many people to visit. I promised her that we would be coming back regularly, and it was my intention to do so. There was no way I could have known that this was the last time we would ever see her.

I don't know exactly when or how Zeak's name became a title: "The Zeakie Dog." It just gradually happened. The people we visited started calling him that. And sometimes they called him "The Pony." Children often asked me if he "came that way." They were referring to his markings. If ever an animal looked as though he had been painted by the hand of God, it was him. He was stunning. He had such a presence. He was so tall and lanky—ninety pounds of lean muscle. His fur was thick and felt like silk. When I walked him, his neck was exactly where my hand fell. It was as if it had been made to fit that way. It was becoming more and more obvious that if there was such a thing as a "soul dog," The Zeakie Dog was it for me. The bond between us was growing stronger and stronger. I am not a religious person, but I am very spiritual. I feel the presence of God all around me. I don't pretend to understand all the pain and suffering in the world. I don't. But something very special and spiritual was happening with me and this dog. I could feel it.

My two boys were very different. From day one, long before The Zeakie Dog came into our life, Lakota clung to me—he stuck to me like glue. He had the kindest and most secure and loving upbringing. Yet he had separation anxiety and when I left the house, he would bark and cry and howl. He never touched a thing, but he was not happy when I left—that was clear. And despite leaving him puzzles with treats, music, chews, etc., it never changed.

The Zeakie Dog would smile at me when I was going out. He had total confidence that I would never abandon him. Perhaps this was because we were never really out of touch. He knew where and how I was at all times—I don't know how, but he did. One afternoon, he was out in the yard and I was in the house. I was sitting thinking and feeling kind of down about something that had happened. A person I thought was a friend had done something hurtful, and I was having a quiet moment of letting myself cry it out. All of a sudden, The Zeakie Dog came flying through the dog door, ran over to me as fast as a dog that size could run in our little house, and started frantically smothering me with kisses. He had somehow picked up, from outside, that I was upset. And that's how it was between us. Our relationship was telepathic—more on his part than mine. This dog was something really special. For a lot of reasons, I was a somewhat battered soul. This dog had been sent to me for a reason. I have always been rather pragmatic. I don't avoid the truth. I deal with it as best I can. I have never been someone who has visions or hallucinations or feels they have psychic abilities. But I could not deny there was something I had never experienced before going on here.

Lakota was a "dog's dog." He had no jealousy of my special connection with Zeakie because he was on a completely different wavelength. He didn't "get" what was between Zeakie and me, or if he did, he didn't have any interest in it. He was all about scents, running, fetching, eating, rolling in the grass, swimming, and retrieving. When we were out on the trails, his training went out the window if he picked up a scent. I could call him till lightning came out of my head. He was busy. He would come to me when he got around to it.

If I called Zeakie in the woods, he would whip his head around and fly to me, jumping over fallen trees. It was a beautiful sight. I loved both dogs with all my heart. But something different was happening with The Zeakie Dog and me. We "got" each other because we were so much alike. It was like he knew the location of every hole in my heart, and exactly how to fill it.

Zeakie had a very evolved sense of humor. When Lakota took off, chasing a quad (a four-wheeled all-terrain vehicle), in the woods one day, I decided I had to get an E-collar for him, to get him to listen in safety-related situations like this one. An E-collar is a remote-controlled collar that emits a warning tone, and gradual levels of electrical stimulation. Despite working with two trainers and a lot of training time, my Lab just wasn't reliable off leash, and I feared he would be run over. When I got the collar and put it on Lakota, The Zeakie Dog smiled and smiled and laughed his head off. He had seen the collars and knew what they were. I could read his thoughts, "Bro, you are SO busted! Now you HAVE to listen. Your days of taking off and ignoring being called are over!"

One thing both of my dogs had was some kind of radar about when I was coming home, if I went out. My husband is a total skeptic. He is a technical/science-oriented person. Yet, time and time again he witnessed that about four or five minutes before I came home—long before they could hear my car—they would both go to the front door and wait excitedly, because they knew I would be home soon. I have had friends tell me their dogs do the same thing. How do they know?

Dogs love to work. They have a serious work ethic, and it is very easy to teach a Lab to do jobs that involve carrying things in his or her mouth. For some time Lakota had been helping me carry in the mail and the groceries. Zeak had observed this, and wanted a job of his own. He had also observed me gathering laundry every morning and putting it in a laundry basket. After it was all collected, I would bring it downstairs to sort and wash. It was a bit of a surprise when I started finding a dog toy in every basket of clothes. Finally, one morning, I saw Zeakie dropping one of his rubber balls into the laundry basket, and realized he was trying to help me do the laundry. Zeak had decided what his job would be, and did it every morning.

In January of that year, I had a dog birthday party to celebrate Lakota's fourth birthday and The Zeakie Dog's second. Two other dogs in our group of friends had January birthdays, too, so we had a great celebration for all four dogs with presents, games, and birthday cake from the dog bakery—a yummy but healthy concoction of sweet potatoes, whole-grain flour, canola oil, bananas, etc.—with yogurt and sour cream icing. All in all, there were eight dogs at the party, and their owners. Everybody had a great time. We played out in the snow with the dogs and came in for dog cake, and people cake, and cocoa, and coffee; and warmed up by the fire. It was the best of times. Had I known what lay ahead, I would have prayed for all I was worth to freeze those moments forever.

Because The Zeakie Dog had grown up with Lakota, he thought he was a Labrador Retriever, and retrieved like a true water dog!

CHAPTER 11

A Disturbing Visit: January 2007

I was trying to make a visit a week to the facilities that the dogs and I were serving, and once in a while, if I had some extra energy, we would slip in an extra visit. My dogs were in demand, and I simply could not do as many visits as the three places I was serving wanted. But when I saw a request in our therapy dog magazine for a local facility, I decided to fit them in—even if just for one time—because I didn't want to ignore their request.

It was Lakota's turn to visit. I only worked one dog at a time. It was too hard to keep my eye on two dogs. I had already grabbed a cup of hot coffee from a woman, just before it was spilled on Zeakie. The woman was very elderly with some dementia, and had gotten so excited when she saw a dog that she forgot the coffee was even in her hand. That incident assured me I was doing the right thing bringing one dog at a time.

I set my navigator for the facility's address, and we were there in about twenty minutes. I walked in and headed for the office I had been directed to. A very friendly woman greeted me, and told me how happy they were to have us. She told me that we would be going to the Alzheimer's unit, and that she would be sending an orderly with me. Since the facility was huge, I was glad they would have someone going with me.

The dogs and I had visited Alzheimer's patients before, so I thought I knew what to expect. When we stepped off the elevator, the orderly headed for the men's wing first. He walked so fast that I could barely keep up with him, and he spoke so little English that I couldn't ask him to slow down.

The men were not in their rooms. They were all milling around in the large hallway, and many of them were big, surprisingly young, strong, angry, and even yelling. For the first time ever in our work, I felt uneasy—in fact, I felt we were unsafe. The orderly was a very small young man, about my size. I doubted he would be able to handle a situation if it got physical, especially with some of these really big, very angry men. He went over to talk to a patient, and we were starting to make contact with a few of the calmer men, when a nurse came over and asked to speak to me. She took me aside and told me to go to the women's side. She asked me not to tell anyone that she had told me to do that, but she was concerned that one of the men might hurt my dog. I thanked her and walked down toward the women's hall. My heart was racing and I just wanted to get Lakota out of there safely. When the orderly caught up to me, I simply told him that the men hadn't seemed very interested so I had moved on. He had no idea what I said, but he didn't try to direct me back, so I just kept on.

The women were mostly in their rooms. We had several nice visits, and Lakota even seemed to be able to pull a few of them out of the spaced-out state they were in when we arrived. We had finished that side of the hall and were crossing over to do the other side, when a well-dressed woman in a wheelchair rolled up to us and approached Lakota. I greeted her and introduced Lakota. Before anyone could move or think, she had grabbed two fistfuls of skin on Lakota's back and was squeezing so hard he started crying. The useless orderly just stood there. I firmly told her to let go, but she had an iron grip on my poor dog's skin, and was hurting him. In desperation I pointed down the hall and yelled, "Oh no—look at that!!!" As the woman turned around to look, she relaxed her grip and I pulled my dog out of her grasp. I was furious that the facility had sent us into this situation, where my dog was not safe, and with a staff member who was not trained and capable to handle situations like this. I told Lakota what a trooper he was, and asked the orderly to escort me out. He looked at me, and I said, "I want to go." That he got, and he led me to the entrance downstairs.

A lot of animals would have attacked under those circumstances. Lakota was a rock, but he did not sign up for this kind of treatment. There was not enough staff in this facility, and patients weren't being managed in a way that was safe. I found it perplexing that there were all sorts of visual amenities, very upscale, even opulent décor—but they were skimping on the most important things. This was the first time I had felt this way in a facility I had visited.

Lakota had gone above and beyond the call of duty, so I took him to a local dog boutique for a special treat: dog "ice cream" made from frozen yogurt with a little honey. He loved it. Then I purchased some of their store-made treats for my boys and took Lakota home.

I had been cooking for both of the dogs for some time, both their food and their treats. There had been two recalls of dog food that involved many deaths, some from renal failure. I had decided, there and then, that my dogs were not going to eat commercial dog food. I educated myself on canine nutrition, and included an additive that covered all the trace minerals, and some other important things that might be missing from a home-cooked diet. I also made their treats, which were as healthy as their food. We were not people of means, but this didn't cost much more than a high-quality commercial dog food. I was making the food in big batches and freezing them in glass containers. I was also making enough for my son's dog, because with both he and his wife working full time, with very long commutes, they did not need this extra chore. At one point I actually injured a tendon in my arm stirring a big batch. At that point, Bill started helping me. But two people couldn't work in our tiny kitchen, so he made the food and I shuttled it downstairs to the freezer. I made the treats, and we had two dogs that were healthy and gorgeous. I was often stopped and asked what I was putting on their coats to make them so shiny. I told the people who asked that I put nothing on their coats—it was what I put *in* the dogs: actual food!

By now it was late in the winter of 2008. Both dogs had just had their checkups and were due some vaccines. I was very careful with vaccines and only allowed one at a time to be given. I researched and agonized over every one. They scared me, because I had heard and read of problems with the vaccines and some of their ingredients, but our lifestyle of hiking every day, and living right on the watershed, with wild animals all around us, tipped things in the favor of boostering. This was right before titering became an option (testing your dog's level of immunity, so you only vaccinate when necessary). That is what I do now, except for rabies, which is mandatory. We finished up all the shots that were due, and the next few weeks were spent enjoying the first hints of spring.

Because The Zeakie Dog had grown up with Lakota, he thought he was a Labrador Retriever. Lakota was a strong swimmer who would swim after balls and dummies thrown out into the lake with a vengeance and a passion. And so did The Zeakie Dog! He would get so excited, he would cry as I prepared to throw his dummy, and tear into the lake after it like a true water dog. Lakota and the other retrievers in the pack could not lose The Zeakie Dog in the water. He was not about to be left behind, so he became a retriever of sorts, by association.

The dogs were so happy. They loved these group walks/group swims, with their dog and human friends. Because of the joy it gave our dogs, we humans pushed ourselves to take these walks every day. It was very beneficial for all of us. I could not have made myself do this on my own, but my love for my dogs gave me the strength to do it, and I was beginning to feel a little better for it.

We had finished our walk one morning and I had grocery shopping to do, so I grabbed my list and left. When I came back almost two hours later, there was blood all over the kitchen floor, and some on the living room rug. Zeakie was on the couch licking his paw. When I looked at it, I saw a gash about three inches long and so deep, I couldn't look any more without feeling queasy. I wrapped it and headed for the vet's.

General anesthesia, and an hour and a half of surgery later, Dr. Weaver told me the cut had gone into the tendon. He said it was a very serious wound, and if Zeakie ripped it open he could sever the tendon. He would have to be crated for weeks and only go out on a leash to relieve himself. He said he had seen wounds like this before: they happened when a dog's foot slid under a chain link fence and the sharp wires sliced the foot as they pulled it out. Epiphany!

Zeak had taken his whole walk on that injury, and hidden it from me. Most dogs hide injuries, and Shepherds especially do it—it is a survival instinct. He had been alone with his terrible wound all the time I was grocery shopping. I now realized that Lakota's injury had been from the fence too. I took Zeakie home, anticipating another ordeal. I held his foot and told him to "leave it," as I had with Lakota. He never once touched it. After the second day, I took the cone off. I knew the wound bothered him. But I also knew he so trusted me that he would do as I asked. I don't know how I could be so sure—I just could. And he never once touched it, whether I was home or not, no cone, no crate.

My son came and put plastic tubing over the bottom of the fence. Then Brian came to visit and piled rocks all around the bottom, so the weed trimmer wouldn't damage the plastic tubing. After stitches, surgery, and Lakota almost losing an eye, our dog yard was finally safe. Let the fence buyer beware.

I want desperately to see what Lakota sees.

CHAPTER 12

The Invisible Spot: After November 13, 2011

It has happened every single night since Zeak has been gone. Lakota goes to the far side of my bed, like he always does, so he can jump on the bed without stepping on me. He used to just jump up and lie down, but not anymore. Now he stares and stares—looking like his eyes are going to pop out of his head—stares at the space between the edge of the bed and the night table, at some invisible spot, about the same height as my pillow.

It's hard to interpret his expression. I see shock, intense scrutiny, and awe. His ears are plastered tightly to the sides of his head. He seems hesitant about getting up on the bed. I have to call him up several times. Sometimes this will last for five minutes or more. When he finally stops staring at the invisible spot and does jump up, he won't lie in the space he occupied for the previous seven years. He will only lie at the foot of the bed—the place where The Zeakie Dog used to sleep. I have to wonder for whom he is saving the space right beside me.

I have looked at that spot in every kind of light...looked at it in the daytime and looked at it at night...looked at it with a flashlight in the dark...looked at it standing, and looked at it kneeling on the floor. I have looked at it when the sun is shining, when it's raining, when the autumn leaves are swirling in the wind, and when the first winter snow is falling. I have looked for three months. I desperately want to see what Lakota sees. I. See. Nothing.

*Lakota loved his new brother,
and his new brother loved him.*

CHAPTER 13

Normal, Sweet Normal: Summer 2008

By now, you are probably wondering if I have any life at all, besides taking care of my dogs. The answer to that is: entirely too much! The fact is, I am overscheduled and booked blind, almost every day. I have friends outside of my "dog friends," and I spend a good deal of time socializing with them. I am an artist and I do work at my calling, as well as playing the guitar and singing. I have a mother—another big dog-lover—that I spend time with as well as a husband, and son, daughter-in-law, and grandson. I have a brother as well, who as you might have guessed, also loves dogs. Dogs have always been important to my family.

I mention this because there is a misconception that people who deeply love their animals are people who are lonely and don't have relationships with human beings. That has actually been studied and found to be untrue. My friends have been my friends for many years and are like an extended family to me. I cannot say enough about girlfriends. They are the glue that holds life together. Life throws lots of hard times at us. What has always gotten me through is the support of my female friends, and I will always be there for them. That's what women do.

As we took our many walks on the trails together, one of the dogs that really grabbed my attention was a senior dog named Ice. Ice was a blue merle Australian Shepherd—a medium-sized dog with black and white and slate blue hair, and ice blue eyes. Around her eyes were black markings that looked like war paint. She was smart and very affectionate, but it was also clear that she could be a fierce little warrior if she needed to protect her flock. The dogs in the group all understood that she was getting on in years, and even the young pups in the group like Zeakie respected Ice and knew not to pounce on her when they played, as they did with one another. No one who looked at her could have imagined how old she was. And though she was twelve years old, Ice still play-bowed (a position a dog assumes with its front end lying down and its back end standing up to signal a desire to play with another dog) and tried to run around with the other dogs. She had her aches and pains, but still longed to play with her friends. Once in a while, she would surprise everyone and have a little romp with her pals, until they all got hot and plunged into the refreshing waters of the lake to cool off.

When you have an older dog you are faced with the fact that dogs live such very short lives. While those of us with young dogs were taking for granted the good times at hand, Ice' owner Erin was walking scared. She knew that time was not on her side. She had lost dogs before, and knew that it was a very painful process. We all liked to take pictures of our dogs, but for Erin—knowing she would need those pictures down the road to help comfort her through a hard loss—the need to take them had become more urgent.

The summer of 2008 was a time that actually passed as "normal." Normal is a beautiful thing! There were no dog disasters. In fact, there were no disasters in our little world, period. The Zeakie Dog tore around the woods and on the trails with his friends, swam like a Lab, and worked as a therapy dog. Lakota was also working as one. He was now an adult: strong, confident, and kind. He loved his new brother, and his new brother loved him. I was managing my own health condition and feeling a little better. Life was good!

The Zeakie Dog had become quite a character. One morning, when he and Lakota were dog-playing and roughhousing, Zeakie was getting noticeably annoyed at Lakota's refusal to back off. So he did something about it: he carefully maneuvered himself into position and lowered his back end and sat on Lakota's head! Surely this was the ultimate indignity one dog could inflict on another. After that, every once in a while, when another dog was aggravating him, Zeak would do this. None of the other dogs in our group ever did this, not even once. It was pure Zeakie Dog, and reserved for special occasions when another dog was being what Zeak perceived as disrespectful. It didn't happen often, but when it did our group would delight in it, saying, "Look! He's gonna do it! He's getting into position…!" And because it was only done when another dog was being really bratty to Zeak, we never intervened. But we did have a good laugh over it.

There was another thing Zeak was doing that puzzled me. Our office was up in the loft, and you got to it by a ladder. Every time I went up there, without fail, two things would happen. Lakota was not happy that I went where he couldn't go. He would lie under the ladder, looking worried and unhappy, and wait for me to come down. Occasionally, if I stayed up too long, he would raise his head and howl like a wolf. He hated it when I was up there. Zeak, on the other hand, would smile his biggest smile at me, and with a big, sweeping motion, use his long, pointy nose to gesture up the ladder. I thought perhaps he thought it was really cool I could go up there and wanted to join me. The reactions of the two dogs were polar opposites.

Because my condition was limiting the amount of walking I could do, I was visiting some of the smaller facilities with my dogs. One particular visit was to a new assisted living facility about twenty minutes from our home. As we started making the rounds in the large common room, Zeakie made it clear that he wanted to visit a particular man, who was sitting leaning over with his face looking down at the floor. As we approached I asked the man, as it was our custom to do, if he would like to say hello to my dog. The man did not respond in any way. Another man who was seated nearby told me that the first man would not speak to, look at, or respond to anyone. He told me that the man did not hear at all, but that he also refused to communicate in any other way with anyone.

While I was talking to the second man, before I could react and stop him, The Zeakie Dog launched a stealth dog attack of rapid-fire kisses on the silent man's downturned face. Much to everyone's surprise, the man put both of his hands on Zeakie's back and started rubbing and scratching in all the right places—places that only someone who had dogs would know about. And as The Zeakie Dog delighted in the massage and butt-rub he was getting, we all saw the man's cheeks bulge and realized that he was smiling. The other people sitting nearby said that was the first time they had ever seen him smile.

After that, whenever we visited there I was sure to give this man extra time with Zeak. I felt this was important since, to my knowledge, Zeak was the only living thing this man interacted with. He made no contact with me, or anyone else at all. But he and Zeak had their own way of communicating, and it got to the point that this gentleman would even get a Zeakie Dance!

Why would He send me this incredible dog, only to take him away?

CHAPTER 14

A Very Close Call: September 2008

Several weeks later, I arose one morning to find Zeakie had huge, golf-ball-sized lumps all over his face. I suspected bee stings. I called ahead, and told the vet's office I was coming in with what might be an emergency—I needed them to assess that. Dr. Weaver had a very busy practice. He saw a lot of animals. Sometimes that was a disadvantage, but on this day it would be an asset. A lot of vets might not have recognized these symptoms, but he knew immediately what was going on. He told me that this was a serious inflammatory reaction from either a disease or a vaccine. The lumps on Zeak's face were huge hives, and he didn't pull any punches: He told me this was beyond anything he felt comfortable handling. He said Zeak might not survive this, but his best chance was with a board-certified veterinary internist.

I could barely process what he was saying. How do you go from healthy, happy, carefree, two-year-old puppy to might-not-make-it, overnight? I thought I must have heard him wrong, so I asked him again, "Did you say he might not survive this?" The vet answered in the affirmative. He told me that dogs had very powerful immune systems. That's why they could do things that would make us seriously ill, like drink from the lake or eat goose poop. And that powerful immune system was now attacking Zeakie's body.

The internist that Dr. Weaver felt was best equipped to handle this was at a place that handled difficult, serious cases that vets referred to them, as well as after-hours emergencies. It was called Animals First, and had a wonderful reputation, but was, of course, more expensive than a regular vet. At this point I was glad I had taken out health insurance for both of the dogs, because I couldn't imagine how we would have been able to pay for this, otherwise. Dr. Weaver had his receptionist make an appointment—a week later was the soonest they could see my dog. Then, Dr. Weaver gave Zeak a shot of a steroid, and gave me steroid pills to hold Zeakie till he could be seen. He told me that he would have lab work back in a day. That would give us more information.

When I got home I was still in shock. How could this be happening to such a young dog? I took such good care of my dogs. They had the happiest lives, the most love, exercise, mental challenges, good, genuine food, and the best medical care I could give them. I had never had a seriously ill dog before. Injuries, yes, but never anything like this. Then I remembered Zeakie was most likely a puppy mill dog, and health issues are common in these dogs—victims of careless, heartless breeding. The people who run these places think nothing of breeding dogs with active diseases of all kinds, even cancer. How ironic that the best dog I ever had was from the most horrible of places.

And so, once again, I got down on my knees, this time to pray for my two-year-old dog's life. He was the most loving, most intelligent, obedient, happy dog I had ever known. He smiled at me all the time! He made hundreds of people happy. If any animal deserved a chance at life, he did. However, I was not going to allow anyone to hurt him. I knew more than I wished to about the terrible suffering of the dogs in puppy mills. As long as I had anything to say about it, no one was going to make this dog suffer again. I would let him go first, no matter how much it broke my heart.

As I said earlier, I am not a religious person, but rather a spiritual one. I talk with God all the time. It is a dialogue that runs in my mind, kind of like a virus protection program runs in the background on a computer. I meditate every day to just be quietly with God. I feel the presence of God many times during my daily activities. I had deeply felt His presence during the whole process of Zeak finding his way to me. Why would He send me this incredible dog, only to take him away?

On the other hand, I was not naive: I knew that bad things happened to good people…and good dogs. I will not pretend to know why this is allowed to be in this world, nor can I pretend to be at peace with it. The injustice here is truly the most troubling spiritual question.

Just around the time I became sleepy and got into bed, Zeakie began to act strangely. He would run up to me in bed looking distressed, then run away. I got up and followed him, and saw him run out the dog door as fast as he could, and run as far away as the fence would allow. Then he ran back to me, looking into my eyes, and then repeating the same sequence, over and over. He did not make a sound.

Because I have a sleep disorder and have a lot of pain at night, my doctor put me on a prescription analgesic to help me sleep. I had taken it right before bed. I was finding Zeak's behavior alarming, but my husband didn't think there was anything that troubling about it. I told him I wanted to take Zeak to Animals First, where the specialist was, because it was after eleven p.m. and our vet was closed. Since I had just taken my pill, I couldn't drive, so I asked him if he would drive us. He told me that he had to get up early for work and that Zeakie was fine. I asked a few more times and expressed my concern that something was really wrong, but Bill wasn't moving. I called the dogs to come to bed with me and Zeak came along, so I thought perhaps Bill was right.

At three-thirty a.m. Zeakie woke me up and this time there was no mistaking the distress in his eyes. By then, my medication had worn off and I could drive. I got his collar and seat belt harness on as fast as I could, and loaded him in the car—which was done with great difficulty—punched the address into my navigator, and headed for Animals First. It wasn't till we pulled into the parking lot that I noticed I was in my pajamas.

When we arrived, Zeakie was reluctant to jump out of my small SUV. He finally did, but he was acting strangely. We walked in and the young woman at the front desk was welcoming, kind, and efficient. I must have looked upset, because she assured me that most of the people who came through their doors at night were in the same shape I was, nor was I the first to arrive in PJs. She told me the emergency vet would see me quickly. A woman who was waiting at the counter came and gave me a hug and told me that the vets there had saved her dog's life, and that they were the best of the best. I thanked her for her kindness, and she said to "pass it on."

The receptionist told me that because Zeak had an appointment the next week, everything had been transferred from Dr. Weaver's records to theirs, so the vet would have all Zeak's pertinent information, including the new lab work, which had come in late that afternoon. A tech came out and brought us to an examining room. The vet, who looked to be in his late thirties or early forties, assured me that they would do everything possible to help my dog. I got Zeakie onto the lift table. The vet raised the table and started feeling and pressing on different parts of the dog's body. Not a peep out of The Zeakie Dog.

The vet looked up and told me that Zeakie was in serious pain. He could tell by the reaction of the muscles when he pressed on them. He said that dogs hide their pain, and Shepherds in particular do, because if predators know they are injured, they will attack them and their herd. He said that Zeak's immune system was attacking his joints, and that the pain was so bad he was going to sedate him. He said that the good news was that because Zeakie had come in as an emergency, he would not have to wait a week; he would be the internist's first appointment this morning at eight a.m.

I expressed concern about leaving Zeak in a cage because of his history, and the vet assured me that Zeak wouldn't be aware of where he was. I could see Zeakie's eyes closing as the vet gave him the sedation. I was in no position to argue. He told me to go home and get some rest—that the internist would call me as soon as he examined Zeak.

I drove home and arrived to the sound of Lakota howling like a wolf! A chill went through me. He ran to the window to look for his brother. I told him Zeak would be back. I knew I wouldn't be able to sleep so I meditated. I knew there were going to be decisions to make and I had to be thinking as clearly as possible. I was really angry at Bill for refusing to drive us earlier, thus delaying getting Zeak help and relief from his pain, so I didn't want to talk to him. But I realized we would both need to be involved in these decisions, so I called and filled him in.

I had barely hung up the phone when it rang again. I had a sick feeling in my gut when I picked it up. It was the internist: Dr. Olsen. He confirmed that my dog was gravely ill—and though he had among the highest lupus and lyme disease readings he had ever seen, we couldn't be sure if the cause of his inflammation was one or both of those diseases or one of his vaccines, causing a reaction that triggered those readings. He said that he needed to put Zeak under anesthesia, and put needles into his joints, to withdraw fluid for testing. He said that and some other tests would give him the information he needed to devise a plan to try to save my dog. When I asked him, he told me that he could not say whether or not Zeak would survive.

I gave him the go-ahead with one stipulation: He was not to cause my dog any pain or stress. All testing was to be done while he was under anesthesia. I told him I would rather lose him because he was given anesthesia to keep him comfortable, than to have him live, but have to suffer. I told him that when he was done I wanted to bring my dog home as soon as possible. He said he would call as soon as Zeakie was coming out of the anesthesia, so I could start the drive there. I hung up, and Lakota and I got into bed, snuggled next to each other. And even though I couldn't sleep, I rested, knowing I would need my strength for what lay ahead.

Molly was a dog in constant motion.

CHAPTER 15

The Snake: After November 13, 2011

It started soon after Zeakie passed. It was a Sunday morning and Lakota and I were waiting for Karen and her dog Molly, to come down the street to meet us for our walk. Finally we saw them down the road. Just as they reached the crossroads at our house, Molly—who usually dragged Karen down the street because she couldn't wait to greet my boys—stopped cold. She was staring at an area right by Lakota and me, but not at us. The look of shock, panic, and confusion on her face caught us all by surprise. For minutes, she refused to move a step. If Karen tried to make her move she would pull back and fight the leash. Frankly, she looked like she had seen a ghost. It took a while, but Karen finally got her to move. We headed for the trail. After that, our walk was normal.

Every Sunday for several weeks after Zeak died, Molly repeated this behavior. Finally, one Sunday morning after it had occurred again, something happened on our walk. We were coming home on the trail that led to our road. Lakota and Molly were about fifteen feet ahead of us on the trail and Karen was behind me, when she said, "Margo, stop!" I knew from her voice something was wrong. When I looked ahead I saw Lakota and Molly turned around on the trail, facing us. They were like two statues—as still as if they were frozen. Then I looked down, and to my horror saw a snake as thick as a banana coiled around Lakota's two front feet like a figure eight, touching them on all sides. Molly was standing right next to Lakota and the snake was also touching the side of Molly's foot. It did not look like a poisonous snake, but it was big enough to inflict a serious and very painful bite. La-

kota's feet were so sensitive he couldn't even stand to have them touched. I could hardly bear to watch.

The minutes went by in slow motion, and still the two dogs did not move a bit. Molly was a dog in constant motion. We had never seen her stand still this long in her life! I tried to stay calm, but I started to lose it—I was terrified the snake would strike. Karen and I were perplexed because the dogs weren't just still, they looked completely calm and disinterested. Finally the snake moved away, leaving both dogs unharmed.

Everything about how Lakota and Molly acted in that situation was totally contrary to the way I would have expected them to act. If they had behaved normally and tried to run or bite the snake, they would have been injured. I believe the dogs had a guardian angel with them—one who knew that danger was coming, and somehow communicated to both dogs exactly what to do to avoid harm. I never feel alone in the woods anymore. Even if Lakota and I are walking alone, I know we are being watched—and guarded. Because we are walking with his shadow.

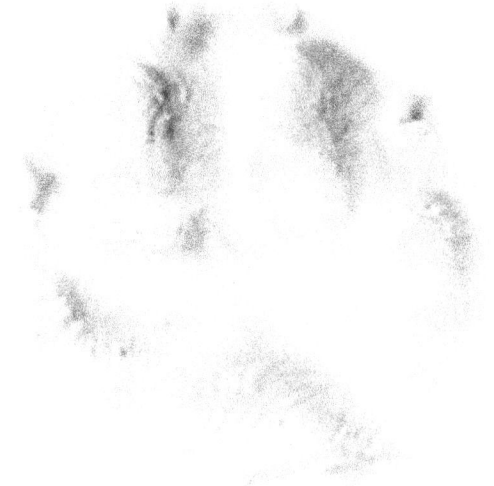

For the next three days, I tended to a depressed, lethargic, but totally sweet dog.

CHAPTER 16

The Aftermath: September 2008

It was close to 3:30 when Dr. Olsen finally called. He told me I could head down to confer with him and then bring Zeak home. I hated leaving Lakota home, but I needed plenty of room on the back seat for Zeakie. I was not at all sure what condition my dog would be in. One of the women from our dog group came with me and drove my truck, because I was too tired to drive safely.

Dr. Olsen was not a warm and fuzzy kind of guy, and he had nothing comforting to say. He told me that Zeak's condition was "guarded." He said that some dogs with this condition would survive, some would not, and some would survive but never be the same again, in that their health would be compromised. He told me that Zeak would be put on 100 mg. a day of the potent steroid prednisone, azathioprine (an immune-altering, anti-cancer drug), large doses of doxycycline (an antibiotic), and prilosec to protect his digestive system from the onslaught of the other drugs.

When I heard how much prednisone my dog had to take, the tears started to flow. I had been on and off this drug for much of my adult life to control my asthma. I weighed forty pounds more than Zeakie. When I was on 60 mg. of prednisone I thought my brain was going to explode and I was ready to rip someone's head off. How was my poor dog going to tolerate this? He didn't understand why he was feeling so awful. He was still a puppy. But it was not as if there were a lot of options here. I took the meds, handed them my credit card, and waited for them to bring my dog out.

The tech led out a dazed and stunned-looking Zeakie Dog. He barely greeted me. I was glad he had been so out of it during his stay here. It showed me that they had kept him sedated. The tech came out with us to help with getting him in my vehicle, but Zeakie was able to get in the truck by himself, motivated by his strong desire to go home.

When we arrived home, I took over the driving, and then drove up the lawn and around to the back gate so Zeakie would not have to walk up stairs. Bill, now home from work, came out to help us and the three of us got a weakened Zeakie dog in the back door. He barely greeted Lakota and went to sleep on the floor in the dining room. I went in the bedroom and prayed for my dog's life.

For the next three days, I tended to a depressed, lethargic, but totally sweet dog. He was ravenous from the massive doses of prednisone he was getting twice a day, but Dr. Olsen had warned me not to let him gain weight, because the extra weight on his inflamed joints could do serious damage. I had to believe my dog was going to make it, so I needed to take care of his joints. But he was begging and pleading with me for food, something he had never done. It was heartbreaking. I called Donna and she told me to go to the warehouse store and buy huge bags of frozen vegetables. She told me to cook them till soft and mushy, and give Zeakie a nice big lunch of this. He was so ravenous, he devoured his extra meal, and thanked me afterward with extra kisses and a failed attempt at a Zeakie Dance. Of course, I had to also give Lakota some, so he began to have veggies for lunch too, and I blessed the warehouse for having organic vegetables in huge bags at a price I could afford.

On the fourth day of this regimen, The Zeakie dog started to come to life again. It was October first, and I saw a hint of a spark in his eyes. By the end of the first week, he was getting up from the floor to a standing position without such a struggle. A few days later he smiled at me for the first time since he had become so ill. He even was getting a little playfully bratty with his brother again.

Zeak was still in a lot of pain from the inflammatory arthritis in his joints, so we hired a certified animal rehabilitationist and massage therapist to work on Zeak at home. She specialized in helping animals recuperate from surgery or serious illness. Zeak relaxed and enjoyed these treatments immensely. I hoped that the pleasure and relaxation would help counter all the pain and stress he had gone through. While she worked on Zeakie, I gave Lakota a belly rub, so he wouldn't feel left out.

Three weeks later we went back for a checkup and blood work. Dr. Olsen was away, so his associate—another internist—was to see Zeak. After the lab did his blood work, the internist came out and told me that he was concerned about "strange" liver readings. He was dropping Zeakie's prednisone dose way down, and wanted to retest in ten days. He was also concerned about the drop in the prednisone dosage, and how that would affect Zeak, but we had no choice if we wanted to save his liver.

For the next two months, that was how it was: manage side effects and change medications, blood tests, a few bouts of serious digestive issues, more meds, and lots and lots of love. Despite all the pain, sickness, weakness, and bumps in the road, The Zeakie Dog never once lost his gentle, loving temperament. He was squeezed, stuck with needles, and had pills shoved down his throat. He had digestive issues at both ends, but never once did he have an accident in the house. He was too proud. He would refuse to come in if he felt like he might get sick. He was beyond a trooper; he was the best, most cooperative, brave, and sweet-tempered patient that he could possibly be. I can't imagine a human being going through what he went through without once complaining, being angry, or thinking "Why me?" I, on the other hand, went through all of those emotions for him.

On December 4, 2008, I gave him his last medications. He was standing strong and proud. He was running around the woods and leaping over trees. I thanked Dr. Olsen for saving my dog. For the first time I saw warmth escape from the man. He said, "He's just the kind of dog I like—a big, calm, beautiful dog." Then he added something ominous: "He's so beautiful on the outside, but the inside…." He shook his head as he said this. But Zeakie was still standing! And as The Zeakie Dog and I fought our way through this ordeal, we received a gift: a bond—a closeness beyond anything I had ever experienced with an animal.

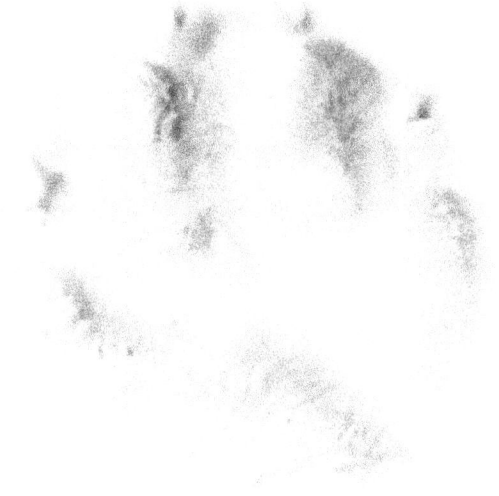

*Zeakie and his little girlfriend even had tug-o-wars,
and Zeakie just held on,
and never pulled too hard for her.*

CHAPTER 17

Celebrating: December 2008

After the close call we had, in December of 2008 we were in a mood to celebrate! We splurged on a very nice Santa outfit for Bill—who grudgingly agreed to play Dog Santa—and made plans for a Dog Christmas Party. We all drew names of the dogs in our group from Santa's hat, and proceeded to buy the neatest toys we could find for each dog's personal taste. Because we all had financial constraints, we set a price limit that we were all comfortable with. We also bought treats from local dog bakeries—there are five in our area—and I baked up a storm of my own recipe dog treats. One of the women made gift bags for each of the dogs with a beautiful photo of the dog on the bag, so we could tell whose stuff was whose. It was kind of like the swag bags that celebrities get when they attend the Oscars, just with different swag!

Mother Nature cooperated and gave us a cold, snow-covered day to add to the Christmasy feeling of the festivities. Bill and I duct taped together two huge, long appliance boxes and made a tunnel for the dogs to run through, and some other games for us to play with the dogs outside. Because it was cold out, we kept a warm fire going and the dog doors open, so people and dogs alike could come in to warm up whenever they wanted.

Everyone brought some kind of food, I cooked up some of my favorite party dishes, and we all pigged out along with our pets. The dog bakery made a beautifully decorated yam cake for the dogs to enjoy, and they gobbled it down with glee. The manager of the bakery ran a little late with the cake and offered to drop it off for us. When she walked in and saw eight dogs, all getting along and playing and being polite, she told us that her own dogs weren't this well behaved, even at home!

Our doggy guests ranged in size from The Zeakie Dog, on down to two little Jack Russell Terriers. Among the group, there were two obvious "couples." One was Erin's dog Ice with a yellow male Labrador Retriever—they were inseparable. The other was The Zeakie Dog with one of the little Jack Russells. They were definitely the odd couple. Whenever they were both in the same vicinity, they were always together. They even took turns chasing each other around, and it drew some stares and comments, this little brown and white dog chasing around an enormous, ninety-three-pound dog! But the two of them had this deal where they shared the power position. It was a joy to watch the two of them tearing around after each other. They even had tug-o-wars, and Zeakie just held on, and never pulled too hard for his little girlfriend.

At the facilities they visited, Lakota and The Zeakie Dog helped people ring in the season too. They each submitted to wearing Santa hats on their visits, and they both learned to "make music" by ringing some bells tied to a small, standing rack. Even though they rang them in no particular sequence, everyone loved it when they did their trick. They brought smiles to faces that hadn't smiled for way too long. Volunteering with therapy dogs is one of the most rewarding things I have ever done.

After the New Year, the winter of 2009 gave us lots of winter wonderlands to hike through. The dogs loved snow. If they got up to a freshly fallen snow, they would tear around the yard in full excitement mode. It was a beautiful thing to watch.

We even went hiking when it was snowing. We had the right gear to keep us warm, and as long as we could see, we did not miss our hikes. When the snow became too deep to walk in, the snowshoers and cross-country skiers would pack it down, and that enabled us to continue. The only time we didn't go was if the snow was too deep or icy to be safe for the dogs. Then we would walk them on leash at a local park that was plowed, being careful to wash the salt off their feet when we came home.

One grey, drizzly, not-so-nice winter day, we ran into Erin and Ice on the trail that went around the lake. Ice was so glad to see her buddies that she shuffled over to Zeakie and play bowed. We were all laughing at how strong her spirit was that she still wanted to play, when she fell over and needed help getting up. It put a sudden stop to the levity, because it smacked us all in the face with the fact that the matriarch of the pack was getting old—very old. It was something we didn't want to think about. Ice was fourteen—substantially old for a dog—and she had experienced a stroke a few months ago. Erin was starting to do serious geriatric dog care. She was devoted to Ice, and stayed home with her most of the time now. Dogs live such short lives that you are never ready for it. And none of us was ready to say goodbye to Ice, least of all Erin and her husband John.

All in all, our dogs made our lives a joy, and we had the satisfaction of knowing we were giving our best friends the best lives we possibly could. Lakota and The Zeakie Dog ran the trails, charged into the lake, and leaped like deer through the drifting snow. They were beautiful, strong, proud, and full of love. It was the best of winters, followed by the best of summers.

The puppy's name was "Cooper," and despite his young age, he had the look of an "old soul" on his beautiful face.

CHAPTER 18

An Entertaining (and Strange) Party: November/December 2009

Fall of 2009 was a classic: crisp, cool air, and brilliantly, colored leaves against a deep blue sky. We all looked forward to our daily walks now, after a hot, humid summer. The dogs were energized and refreshed, and tore around the woods in a joyous celebration of the fact that they were no longer uncomfortable in their thick, black fur coats.

One morning, on our way to the lower trail around the lake, we saw a woman standing in front of her house with a black blob next to her. As we approached, the blob—featureless from a distance—took on the form of a black Lab puppy. When we arrived in front of the house, I called out, "What a beautiful baby!" The woman introduced herself as Elaine, and after introductions all around I asked her if her puppy had all its shots yet. Elaine said they were not quite done. I told her that to protect the puppy, we should take a rain check on dog hellos until the shots were complete, but added that in the future we would love a play date. Both of my boys were very good with puppies, and enjoyed playing with them. We agreed to get in touch as soon as the puppy had all his shots, and grew a little bit more. The puppy's name was Cooper, and despite his young age he had the look of an old soul on his little face.

The time for our annual Christmas party was approaching, and we were beginning to make plans. I was trying to think of what we could do to top last year's party, when I ran across an article in the newspaper's pet column. It was about an animal communicator, a.k.a. animal medium, who worked with problem animals, to help pet owners and trainers resolve problems that would not yield to normal training methods. She also did private and group readings of animals.

At first I was skeptical—I knew that most people who claim to have this gift, don't. However, I had a firsthand experience, years back, with a woman who truly did have this gift, with human beings. She was up in New England and I accidentally bumped into her on a trip there. She told me she was going to do a reading for me, and that no money was to exchange hands—she had a message for me.

I was intrigued, especially when she told me that she was being directed to do this, and she was not going to charge me. I was thirty years old, and had just lost my fifteen-year-old sister to a series of medical mistakes. The woman did a reading, with messages from my sister, letting me know she was fine. She told me that my sister, who had been a gifted pianist, now played both the piano and flute—and that there would be a sign when I returned home, so I would know she was OK, and that this was for real.

The woman then went on to identify every deceased member of my family, by describing unique, very specific personality traits that no one who didn't know each of these people could know. She told me that my grandmother on my mother's side was very excited because soon she would have her son Julius with her. When she came up with my uncle's actual name—and so unusual a name—I almost fell off the chair I was sitting on!

We knew no one in common. There was no internet then. She did not know I was coming. I did not speak a word, so no clues for her. She didn't even know my name. Three days after I arrived back home, I got a call from my mom. She told me that she had received a phone call from a woman whose daughter had been awarded, at her high school graduation, the scholarship for performing arts that had been established in my sister's name. She had heard about my sister, and wanted to invite my parents to their daughter's—are you ready for this—*piano and flute recital!* I could barely talk to explain to my mom why this was so amazing. Two months later, *my uncle Julius passed away.* Yes, there were people who really had this gift!

My little flashback made me more intrigued at the thought of hiring the woman in the article to "read" our dogs. However, when I brought up the idea in our dog group, one of the women in the group said that she knew someone who did this, and she recommended we hire this person instead. Since she could actually give a personal recommendation, and she assured us this woman was the real deal, we went ahead with the plan, and hired her. Her rates were reasonable, and we all chipped in.

The day of the party, we played outside with the dogs, came in for goodies and Dog Santa gifts, and then eagerly awaited the "animal psychic." She was a little late, which only added to the suspense, and when she arrived, the guys—who up till now had made it clear that they thought this was goofy—immediately became intensely interested in this woman. It wasn't because of any psychic gifts she had…it was due to other gifts. To put it succinctly: she was hot!

The alleged psychic had long, platinum blonde hair, and was attired in skin-tight, very low rise jeans, and an equally skin-tight leopard print sweater that didn't quite reach the jeans. The neckline of the sweater was a very low v-neck. Her large breasts were squashed together, and jacked up by some marvel of modern engineering, to the point that we were all wondering if they would suffocate her. As she did her readings, she bent over holding, petting, and talking to the dogs, and getting into all sorts of provocative positions. We might as well have hired a stripper! The only amazing thing that took place that afternoon was that her breasts didn't fall entirely out of her sweater.

One of the dogs in the group, sadly, was dying of heart problems. Her reading of the dog was one of "good health and stamina." She made a couple of comments that could be attributed to lucky guesses, but otherwise failed to dazzle…the women. The guys, however, were totally engaged and entertained—even "Dog Santa," who usually had the attention span of a gnat with social things—managed to stay focused on the alleged psychic. She finally hustled her jingle bells out of there, and then we were all able to have a good laugh about it, after telling the guys how transparent they had been. We ended our conversation with some pig noises for effect!

Even if the alleged animal psychic was a disappointment, a good time was had by all. There was an undeniable gathering of clouds over the dog group, however. One dog was having heart issues, and Ice was about to turn fifteen, and beginning to struggle with mobility. We all knew, but never discussed, that hard times were not far around the next bend in the road for our pack.

Lakota, Shy, and Zeak waiting for Santa.

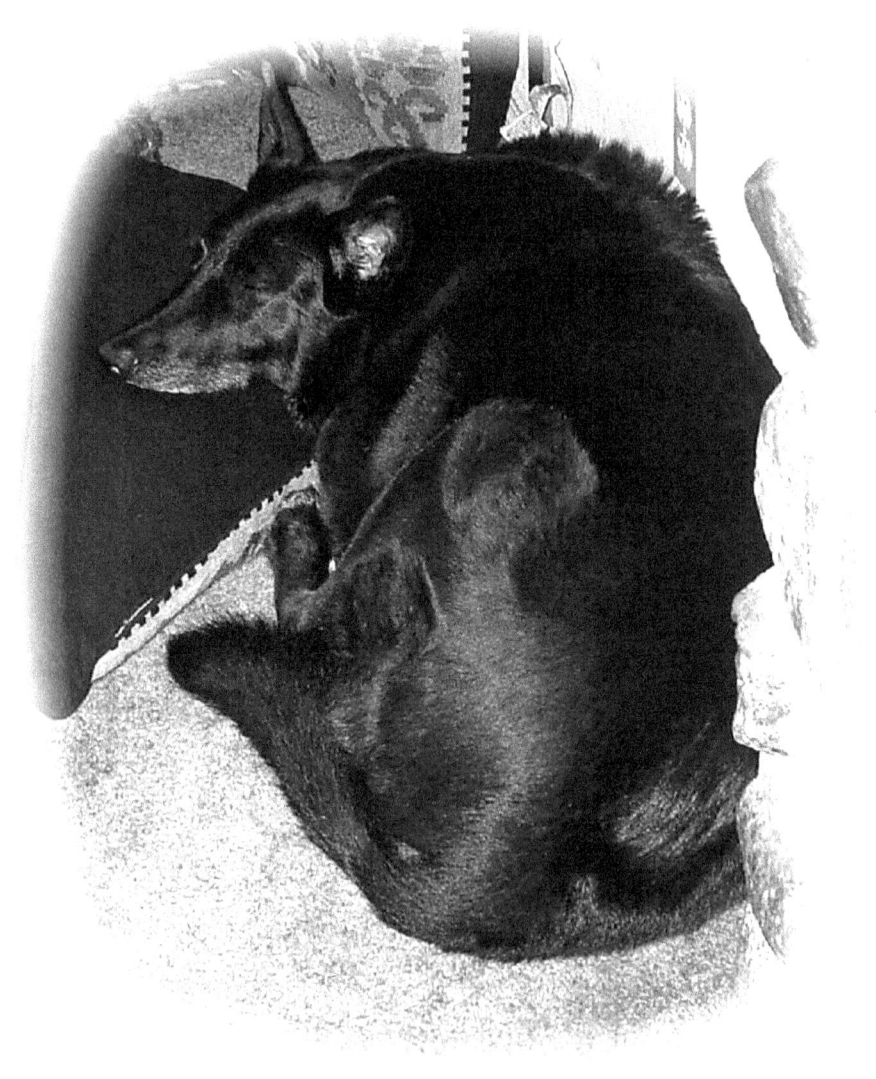

Zeak made a space right next to me by moving a floor pillow that was leaning up against my chair.

CHAPTER 19

Another Visit: After November 13, 2011

It is late in the evening, and Bill and I are watching TV in the living room. Lakota is sound asleep on the couch. For no apparent reason, Lakota is jolted awake—startled by something. He is aroused so suddenly that his abrupt movement distracts Bill and me from the TV, and we turn our heads to look at Lakota. Once again, Lakota looks startled, shocked, and amazed. He is intently staring at something to the left of my chair, on the floor right next to me. This goes on for three or four minutes or so. Then his eyes follow something from that spot, across the living room, and into the hallway. Lakota jumps off the couch and pursues whatever it is into the hallway, and then, into my room. I follow him to find him on the far side of my bed, staring at the invisible spot.

The last few weeks of his life, Zeakie wanted to be as close to me as possible. As I watched TV in the evening, he couldn't lay in front of me, because the recliner was back and the footrest was in his way. So, he made a space by moving a floor pillow that was leaning up against my chair, so he could lay to the left of my chair, on the floor right next to me.

The dogs walked till they got to the lake, and stayed in the water to cool off as long as they could.

CHAPTER 20

The Beginning: July 2010

By the time summer came, we were ready to celebrate Molly and Shy's birthdays. It had been a brutally hot summer. The heat had started early in the spring, before there were even leaves on the trees, so there was no shade, and it did not let up. The dogs were not running around on the trails. They walked till they got to the lake, and stayed in the water as long as they could to cool off. Even that didn't help a lot, because the lake was so warm that it was barely refreshing. Then they walked home, slowly.

It was on a Saturday—July 10, 2010—that we had decided to celebrate the summer dog birthdays. Donna was bringing three of her dogs to join Lakota, Zeak, Shy, and Molly for the event. And one of our neighbors was coming with a dog they had rescued, that my boys really liked: a Bloodhound mix named Jethro. Another neighbor was also attending with her dog, Charlie, a huge Great Dane mix, who was very fond of Lakota. I had purchased real agility equipment (a tunnel, poles to weave through, a hoop to jump through, and a hurdle) for the dogs, and they enjoyed playing with it, especially the long tunnel. I filled a kiddy pool with cold water to help cool the dogs off, and had plenty of water bowls scattered around our shady yard.

One of the dogs Donna had brought was a dog from her rescue named Baxter. He was a grey poodle mix who was blind. He had been born that way, and we were all amazed at how well he got around. He pranced with his front paws out ahead of him and used them as feelers. If he felt stairs he stopped and waited for a human to give him a lift.

Halfway through the party, we brought the dogs inside to cool off and rest in the air conditioning. We waited for a while to be sure they were cooled down, and then everybody gathered around the table and sang, "Happy Birthday," and passed out dog bakery cake and cookies. The dogs all patiently waited their turns as we passed out cake for them. They went absolutely nuts over these dog bakery cakes, but were so polite that it was really heartwarming.

I noticed, when we were outside, that Zeakie was often taking breaks from running, but it was unbearably hot and he had the thickest coat of all the dogs, and it was black as well. He also had a German Shepherd's downy undercoat. It served him well in winter, but in the heat it was a real detriment. He had the option of going into the air conditioning, but he wanted to be with his friends. And he cooled off with his feet in the pool when he needed to. He was four years old now, and Lakota was six. They were adult dogs now, so they weren't going to be running around like puppies in this heat. For these reasons, Zeakie's slowing down a little at the party did not raise any red flags.

There are moments, when looked back upon, that are like a freeze frame in time. One of those moments was about to happen: Towards the end of the party, Zeak was lying down in a corner of the lawn near the house where it is shady, and I noticed Jethro standing nearby, staring at, and barking at Zeak. Over and over, we heard the husky bark of a hound, accompanied with a "roo." It struck me as odd, because Jethro was the quietest dog in the pack. He was timid and quiet and sweet-tempered. But he was not stopping and he looked and sounded upset. He and Zeak were pals—they got along very nicely, and he had never acted like this. He just stood there and kept barking and barking until, concerned that he was disturbing the neighbors, his owners took him away.

What I didn't know was that Jethro, a scent hound, had a terrible secret; he knew something about my dog that even I did not. Something his extremely sensitive nose could smell. Something unthinkable. Something unspeakable. A silent, relentless killer had taken possession of Zeakie's body, and soon, very soon, it would make its presence known. And when it did, nothing in our world would ever be normal again.

On Wednesday morning, July 14, 2010, we walked as usual, and took a quick dip in the lake. Everything was normal.

CHAPTER 21

Our Foe Revealed: July 2010

On Wednesday morning, July 14, 2010, I walked my dogs on the trails, as I did every morning. A forty-five minute walk, with a quick dip in the lake. Everything was normal; the trails were normal, the lake was normal, the dogs were normal. When we got back, I changed into my town clothes and drove to the post office, round trip: forty-five minutes. When I returned home, I knew the minute I walked in the front door that something was wrong, because no dogs came to meet me. I walked through the house to be greeted by the following sight: Zeak was on the kitchen floor lying on his side. Lakota was standing over him, guarding his brother. He was also blocking my view of Zeak's head.

When I walked around to look at Zeak and see what was going on, what I saw almost caused me to faint. Zeakie's head was blown up on one side to the size of half a soccer ball! His whole face was distorted by the enormous swelling. I knew I had to stay calm to help him. I took a deep breath, let it out, and told him I was going to get our car and help him. I ran out front, jumped in, and drove on the lawn around to the back door—the easiest, shortest way, with the least stairs—-to get him into the vehicle. I told Lakota he had to stay home. He backed off, and offered no protest. He, too, knew that something was terribly wrong. I put on Zeak's harness because his collar wouldn't fit on his swollen head. He could barely get up. I had to get him into the back of our small SUV, and somehow he and I found the strength to get him in there.

I drove down the driveway, turned on my hands-free speaker phone, and voice dialed Dr. Weaver's office. When the receptionist answered, I told her I was coming in with Zeak as an emergency. I told her what I had come home to, and wondered if this could be a poisonous spider bite—I had never seen anything like this. My heart sank when she told me Dr. Weaver was away. She said that there was a covering vet there, however. I asked her if the covering vet was someone really good, because, since it was an emergency. I could also go to Animals First. She said that this vet had helped her dog with a heart problem successfully, and that she thought she would be fine. I thanked her and hung up. I was not convinced—an unknown vet—I just wasn't sure. But Dr. Weaver's office was closer and I needed help fast, so I made the decision to go there. But I would have felt better if Dr. Weaver had been there.

When I arrived at the vet's, I got Zeak out of the car; and when he saw he was at the vet's, nervous adrenaline gave him the strength to walk in. The covering vet, Dr. Saige, had a very nice manner. I asked her what could possibly do this. I told her Zeakie liked to chase bugs and asked her if a poisonous spider could do this. She said she had no idea what it was, but that she was going to try to find out. I suspect she could have made a pretty good guess what was wrong with my dog. But she was being kind—she didn't want to give me news like that without a biopsy. At least, that's what she told me months later.

She told me that the lymph nodes in my dog's back legs were swollen: she put my hand on them and I could feel two lumps the size of ping-pong balls. A tech came in to assist. They took blood, and they punctured Zeakie's neck, right into the swelling, with a huge needle, twice. He cuddled his head into my chest and closed his eyes during all of this, and

I stroked and held him. Then they gave him a shot of antibiotics and a shot of prednisone. Since the vet didn't know what was wrong without the tests, she was trying to cover every contingency.

And then Dr. Saige gave me a bottle of prednisone to continue. She said it would get the swelling down. And it did. I had no clue what was wrong with Zeakie, but the rest of the week, Zeakie got better. The swelling went down as he got more and more prednisone into his body. By the weekend, we were going for walks, although I had shortened them because Zeak seemed tired. What I didn't know was that we were wasting precious, precious time, because inside Zeak's body a wildfire was spreading.

Sunday night, my son Tom dropped off my grandson and granddog to stay a few days. On Tuesday morning, almost a week after I found Zeak on the kitchen floor, my cell phone rang as my grandson and I were heading for the trails with Lakota, Zeak, and Shy. I asked my grandson to hold all three dogs' leashes, and fished my phone from my pocket.

It was Dr. Weaver, back from vacation. He did not mince words. He said, "Margo, Zeak has cancer." I leaned on a nearby tree to hold myself up. "What do you mean he has cancer?" I asked, "He's only four years old—how could he have cancer—what cancer?"

Dr. Weaver told me that Zeak had lymphoma. I asked him how serious it was. When he told me Zeak could be gone in about two weeks if we didn't intervene, I dropped to the ground to avoid falling there. He told me that the only chance Zeak had was: if he could be put into remission with chemotherapy, we could buy him some time. He said that chemo was not done like it was with people—it wasn't so hard on dogs, because they didn't give it at a level to cure the dog. The suffering it would cause would be unethical, since the dog did not choose to undergo it. Instead, they used it to buy the dog time and make him/her feel better. And it could buy us quality time, *if* we could get him into remission. He told me that he knew the person who could do it, if anybody could, and he would call her and try to get her to see Zeak immediately, if I wanted to go ahead with this. He warned me that the treatment would be very expensive. Feeling confident in my preparedness, I told him I had insurance.

My head was reeling. I asked him if I had time to think about it. He said, "No. He's stage IV a/b." I asked him what that meant. He said, "It is a cancer rating scale that is used to describe the stages of cancer. Stage IV means that the cancer has advanced and spread to the liver and spleen. Substage a/b means that the patient feels well in some ways and does not in others." I asked him what the end stage was. When he said stage V, I said, "Please call her."

Because we needed the tests to really know what was wrong with Zeak, he had been given prednisone, in case this was some kind of allergic/inflammatory reaction. After the biopsy came in with the shocking news that my dog, who was only four years old, had a deadly cancer, we were behind the eight ball. The cancer had an extra week to spread, because that's how long it takes those tests to be done. It had spread to his liver and spleen. In addition, because he had been given prednisone, he had less of a chance of getting a remission. Prednisone is actually used in some of the cancer treatment protocols, but if it is started before chemotherapy, it reduces the chance of getting a remission. But who could have imagined a four-year-old dog with this? I didn't know cancer—I had never even met it. I only knew of it. I was about to have a crash education.

The next day, I had an appointment with the renowned Dr. Kara Seiford. What I didn't know yet, was that there was normally a wait of over a month to see her. I found that out months down the road, from someone in her waiting room. But we didn't have that kind of time. This particular cancer, lymphoma, is a silent killer that will take down a healthy, big dog, start to finish, in a few weeks. In some cases, it can kill in days!

So, Dr. Weaver called Dr. Kara Seiford and asked her to fit us in. I have no idea what the conversation was that took place, but I suspect he told her how much I loved my dogs, and how thorough I was with their care. And because he cared enough to go to bat for my dog, and because she had a heart, she fit us in the next day, during her lunchtime.

A week after his first treatment, The Zeakie Dog smiled when I put his leash on, and we took a lovely walk!

CHAPTER 22

To Fight or to Say Goodbye: July 2010

That night, I explained to Bill, speaking as well as I could through my tears, what the situation was. To my surprise, tears found their way down his face too. There wasn't much that moved my husband, but The Zeakie Dog had clearly gotten to him. We agreed that we could not make a decision until we heard what this treatment would entail. We were on the same page that there would be no suffering for The Zeakie Dog. We would not allow it—we would let him go before we would put him through a horrible ordeal. We also had no idea about the cost of this. All questions would be answered the next day. I told Bill to go to work because we might need his vacation days down the road. Zeak was a big boy. I might need help handling him later on.

That night I got zero sleep. My overactive brain kept producing images of frail, grey, emaciated-looking people with bald heads and hollow eyes, hooked up to IV's in hospital rooms, holding basins to throw up in. I had seen images like this on TV shows. It was bad enough to have to make a decision to go through that to save a human life. At least a human knew *why* they were suffering…knew they were going through this to try and save their life. From what Dr. Weaver had said, saving Zeakie's life wasn't even an option—all we could hope for was to maybe buy some time for our four-year-old dog. And it was a big maybe.

Dr. Seiford was at Animals First, so it was a familiar road that Lakota and Zeakie and I travelled the next day. I had brought Lakota along for support, for Zeakie—and for me too. I needed my rock. As soon as we arrived, we were ushered into Dr. Seiford's office.

I don't know what I was expecting a renowned veterinary oncologist to look like, but Dr. Kara Seiford took me by surprise. She was young and beautiful with dark hair, dark, warm eyes, and a smile that could light up a heart that was in a very dark place. I introduced myself and my dogs and then proceeded to lose it. She came over and put her arms around me and gave me a long, silent hug. I composed myself and calmed down. We got Zeakie on the lift table and, after first talking to him and stroking him and making him as comfortable as he could be at a vet's, she proceeded to examine him. I put Lakota in a down/stay in the corner. After she had looked Zeak over and felt his lymph nodes, a tech came in and took Zeakie to do some blood work.

Dr. Seiford gave me a sheet of paper. On it were several treatment protocols, and what the odds and time outcomes were for each choice. The very best treatment protocol offered remission varying from one year, for 85% of dogs, to three years for 20% of dogs. And that was usually attained by dogs whose cancer was caught in the early stages. Unfortunately that was not my stage IV a/b Zeakie. She never mentioned the prednisone. I found that out later as I educated myself about this disease. As I mentioned earlier, prednisone given before chemotherapy reduces the chances of a remission. Down the road it is part of the protocols, but it should not be given before chemo. Unfortunately, we didn't know we were dealing with cancer till the tests came back.

Now, I questioned her about what this treatment would be like for my dog. She told me that 85% of dogs have no side effects at all from chemotherapy. The ones that do can usually have their side effects managed. I couldn't imagine this. Again, the image of the suffering human patient came into my mind.

We decided to move our discussion to an empty part of the waiting area, where we had more room to lay out papers. I was finding this choice—whether or not to try chemo—agonizing, when something caught my eye coming in the front entrance. A magnificent Great Pyrenees was prancing across the room, literally dragging his owner along. His coat shone like pure silk, thick and white as snow. Dr. Seiford asked if she could excuse herself for a minute and went to briefly talk with the woman with the giant white dog. Then she came back and said she was going to get Zeak and bring him out so he could be with us while we finished talking.

As soon as she left, the owner of the huge, white dog came over and asked if her dog could say hello to Lakota. While Lakota and her dog were saying hello, she asked me if Lakota was sick. I told her that it was my other dog who was ill, and briefly explained. At that point she gestured at her beautiful dog and told me that he had been getting chemo from Dr. Seiford for almost two years. She said he also had lymphoma and that he was living a very normal life. This robust, strong, energetic dog had lymph cancer? That did it. My decision was made. I was not going to let my four-year-old dog, who had fought to be with me, and fought for his life once before—a dog with whom I had a connection like no other—go down. Not if I could give him more quality life and time…time to spoil him, feed him his favorite foods, play with him, and love him. Time with his adopted brother, who also loved him. As long as the treatments themselves weren't painful or traumatic. Dr. Seiford returned with Zeak and I expressed my concern about the treatments again.

She assured us that they weren't at all traumatic. Everything would be done on an outpatient basis. We would bring Zeak there and he would have blood drawn and tested each time to be sure his immune system was strong enough to have the treatment. Then he would go into a special room that was outfitted to do chemo, and there he would get a shot in one of his leg veins. The whole thing would only take a few minutes, and after that, he could go home.

It would be every week for a while. Then it would spread out to every few weeks. Down the road there would be other methods, none of them painful or traumatic. Some were even pills that I could give him at home. There were numerous different protocols, because the cancer would find a way around the one in use after a while, so every month or so we would have to change and alternate. It was as if the cancer had intelligence. It had to be outwitted and out-maneuvered. My mind was made up—we would fight for as long as Zeakie was feeling well…as long as he could enjoy life.

It was now time to ask what this would cost. I think by now you have the idea that we are not people of means. So when I was told what this would cost, my jaw dropped. By far, most of the cost was the medications. The vet fees were modest. I told her that I wanted to move forward. She gave me an idea of what we would need to get through a year or so of treatment, if we were lucky enough to get a remission. I asked her if we could start now. She said that if we were going to do this, we had to. And so I committed, not knowing how I would pay for this after my insurance maxed out, but knowing I would find a way.

So, the battle began, and The Zeakie Dog had his first treatment. He came out in minutes. I filled out and signed an insurance form, handed the receptionist my credit card, and we all headed home. When we got home, I took Zeak and Lakota for a short walk to the dam. I wanted to keep my dog as happy as possible. His immune system would be under assault. I had to keep his spirits up, but also be careful of exposure to contagious diseases.

Then I went into the house to call up my pet insurance company, only to get more bad news. Yes, cancer was covered, but the maximum allowed would cover only a very small portion of the cost of Zeak's treatment. Bill and I talked it over. We decided to use the home equity line we had to cover Zeak's bills. There was nothing we could do to our house that could even come close to giving us the joy that more time with The Zeakie Dog could give us. We did the paperwork and had the funds put into a savings account. I called our credit card company and asked them if there was any way we could get points for vet bills. They switched us to another card type, and the points we got paid for a chemo treatment and then some.

And then, I had a talk with God. I told him that if ever a dog deserved life, it was this one. I asked him to please intervene and save our Zeakie Dog. I prayed for remission. I prayed for a cure, knowing there was none. I had read about stem cell transplants working, but it was a terrible ordeal to put a dog through, followed by many long weeks of solitary confinement. And after all that, a 50% death rate. I pictured Zeak going through this horrible chemo, which it was—like that for humans—then weeks, no, months of loneliness. Then dying alone, thinking I abandoned him. No! So, I prayed for a miracle. I prayed for…normal.

There are always those who feel a need to judge others. Some people are critical of animal owners spending serious money on an animal they love. We live a very modest lifestyle with a small carbon footprint. Our house is under a thousand square feet. My husband's car has 175,000 miles on it and mine over 100,000. They are both gas efficient. We chose to do this and keep our small house and our old cars. Some of these same people will spend double or triple what we would be spending on our dog on a luxury car and live in a gigantic house that wastes resources. And then turn around and criticize us for taking care of a living thing that loves and is loved and is only four years old.

Another thing that those who criticize animal lovers who treat their pets with cancer should know, is that many of the strides in effective human cancer treatment have occurred because of successes in animal cancer treatment. Dogs have ninety-seven percent the same DNA as humans, so their medicines are our medicines. They are serving in the front lines in this battle.

I had not been able to eat much of anything since Dr. Weaver had told me Zeakie had cancer. I had lost eight pounds in two weeks. I couldn't stop crying. I couldn't sleep. I went to therapy and my therapist told me this was called "anticipatory grieving," and it would actually make it easier at the end because the grieving process would have been started. The only thing that finally snapped me out of it was Donna reminding me what my pain was doing to Zeak. So I squashed it down and put on a happy face for my Zeakie Dog. I decided that, despite what my therapist said about it making it easier later, I would not grieve my dog while he was still with me, and ruin the time that we had left together.

Since we had gotten his diagnosis, Zeakie had gone downhill fast. Every morning we would get ready for our walk, walk out the gate, and Zeak would look at me and turn around to go back home. He loved his morning hike more than anything, but he was too weak to go for even a short walk. A week after his first treatment—one day before our trip for his next one—The Zeakie Dog smiled at me when I put his leash on, and we took a lovely walk to the dam. It was about one fifth of our usual walk, but we were on the trails again, and he was free to sniff and walk around and enjoy his beloved woods. And, best of all, he was feeling better!

The next week we went for his second treatment. When Dr. Seiford walked out of the examining room towards me, she was smiling from ear to ear. I got up to greet her and we hugged. Then she said, "He is responding beautifully—by next week I expect him to be in full remission! He is almost there now." I thanked her, hugged her again, and cried tears of joy. I didn't know how she had pulled this off with all the odds stacked against us, but somehow she had! And when the next week came, true to her word, Dr. Seiford had The Zeakie Dog in full remission.

And when the next week came, true to her word, Dr. Seiford had The Zeakie Dog in full remission!

CHAPTER 23

A Visit in My Room: After November 13, 2011

It is late in the evening on a Friday night. I am reading in bed. Something catches my eye to my left, right where the invisible spot is that Lakota stares at every night. And, strange as this sounds, due to Lakota's behavior, I am beginning to wonder if this spot is some kind of opening/portal between two realms that Zeakie uses to go back and forth.

What has caught my eye is a shadowlike form. I use the term "shadowlike" because it reminds me of a shadow, but I have never seen one like this before. It is not flat; it is three-dimensional. It is a rounded, featureless, oblong shape, about three feet wide, and two and a half feet high... roughly the size of Zeak's body, if viewed from the side. It glides—about three feet off the floor—on a horizontal path from the invisible spot, past the footboard of my bed, where it disappears. Lakota is in a deep sleep, snoring, and has not moved at all.

I immediately try to reproduce this "shadow" by changing positions, moving my hands around, and anything else I can think of that would make a moving shadow where nothing is moving, even though I know very well what it is. I was not moving. Lakota was not moving. He was asleep beside me to my left, right in my sight line, so I would have seen it, if he had moved. No one else was there to create a shadow. Our street is a dead end, and no one had driven by. I try many times, but nothing I can do even comes close to reproducing the "shadow." Anyway, it wasn't a shadow. It was three-dimensional. I know what it was. I know who *it was.*

The Zeakie Dog was feeling better and better every day.

CHAPTER 24

The Gift of Cancer: August 2010

When the dream begins, I am out on the lake alone, in a kayak. The water is as smooth as glass. It is still, quiet, soundless. Suddenly a black snake/dragon thing's head splashes up out of the water. I smash it down as hard as I can with my paddle—smash it again and again, until it disappears beneath the surface of the water. All becomes still again. The surface of the lake returns to glass. It is an uneasy calm. I know it will rise again. I will not rest. I will be watchful, and when it rises up I will beat it down again, and again, and again…and then I wake up.

The Zeakie dog was feeling better and better every day. By the time he was in remission he was acting the way he had before he became sick. I called up Donna and filled her in. She told me that shepherding breeds were very sensitive in every way, including to medications, and to keep a close eye on Zeak. Of course, I assured her I would. All in all, things were very close to normal except for one thing: I knew.

I knew that Zeakie had cancer. I knew that for however long the battle lasted, the reality was that barring a miracle, we would lose the war. And knowing that changed everything. Every morning when I was loading the dishwasher, Zeakie would come into the kitchen and want his butt—his lower back near the top of his tail—rubbed. He l-o-v-e-d that! He asked for it often, and I usually accommodated him, unless I was doing something like the dishes, and had wet hands. Then I would tell him, "Not now—later."

Cancer was the end of that. I now cherished every single second with my dog. If he wanted his butt rubbed he got it, no matter what I was doing. I knew there would be a time, down the road, when I would give just about anything to be able to give him a butt rub—to feel his silky fur under my hands and see his wiggle of pleasure. It was that way with rubbing his ears, too. That had an almost hypnotic effect on Zeakie. He would close his eyes and drift off into some realm of delight. Those ears were as soft as a horse's nose. I loved to touch them as much as he loved to have them touched, and nothing was more important than that.

There was nowhere else I wanted to be. I wanted to drink in every second with him, relish it, and thank God for it. And that was the gift of cancer: It took me out of my rat-race schedule and focused me on each moment I had left with my dog. I gave him long belly rubs. He and Lakota and I took beautiful walks in the woods, without worrying about the time.

About five weeks into remission, we took our weekly Sunday walk with Molly. Molly was a Golden Doodle: a Golden Retriever/Standard Poodle cross. She was a big dog, close to Zeak's size, and seemed to have unlimited energy. She was quite a handful. Her owner Karen and I met through the dogs, and had become friends. Zeak and Molly had met when they were puppies, and right from the beginning, sparks flew! Their relationship was friendly competition! They ran like the wind, and Molly didn't like it if she didn't come in first. They would take off and be neck and neck and then a black blur named Lakota would pass them both. Not many dogs could stay with Lakota in the short run—he was like a Quarter Horse. Molly, upset because he was ahead of her, would start barking. When Lakota ran out of gas, Zeak would move to the front, and she would get even more upset. Finally when Zeak ran out of gas, Molly—who never ran out of gas—would move back to the front. Their tear through the woods sent branches and leaves flying in every direction, uprooted small saplings, and sent chipmunks and squirrels running for their lives.

For the past four weeks during this Sunday walk, Zeakie had been staying at my side. But on this day, he took Molly on, and the three of them went back on their wild tear. Karen and I just watched and marveled at "stage IV a/b" leaping over fallen trees and stretching out his long, strong body in a full run. "No one who looked at that dog would know there was a thing wrong!" said Karen. And it was true. Zeakie looked like a young buck in his prime.

Still, I was concerned about the effects of all the chemicals going into his body. I decided to consult with a holistic vet for nutritional support. I had been doing a lot of research about holistic treatments, and thought it couldn't hurt to add that to our arsenal. I also wanted the vet to go over what we were cooking for the dogs, and see if that could be improved upon.

So I got a holistic vet on board too. He made some changes in Zeakie's food, and started him on a regimen of supplements that challenged my ability to keep up with it all. I couldn't possibly remember it all, so I made charts and checked off what I gave him. There were times, with both regimens underway, when I was giving Zeakie a total of sixty-one pills, capsules, supplements, herbs, and liquids a day! Most I gave him in his food, but some I had to administer by shoving them down his throat. The shocking thing was that he so trusted me, he would open his mouth and relax his throat to make it easy for me.

Of all the things I had to give him, the hardest was the home chemo. I was happy to give it to him because it meant he would live and that he didn't have to have a needle stuck in him. But it was disturbing to have to put on nitrile gloves before even touching something that I was going to make him eat. But again, the trust—he made it easy.

It was very important that Zeak drink a lot with the home chemo or he could get a bladder infection. He also had to go out every half hour or so to urinate, so the chemical did not stay in his bladder long. I did not leave the house for anything those days. The day before, I boiled some beef shank bones in a huge pot of water and made broth. That way, I got Zeak to drink loads of yummy beef broth on home chemo day, with no chemicals or salt in it. He drank and peed all day, and into the night. And so did Lakota, because, of course, I had to give him some too. Thus Zeak never had a problem with bladder infections.

Summer gave way to autumn. The leaves just seemed brighter that year. I had my boys that I loved so, and every day was a gift. More and more I was taking pleasure in the simplest things. The dogs loved the cooler weather, and ran and played and swam in the lake. It was a beautiful time. I was so very grateful to have my Zeakie Dog.

At some point during the fall, Zeakie got sick from one of his treatments. He threw up a few times and I took him to Animals First. The vet on duty, a lovely young woman, gave Zeak a couple of shots that put a stop to it. She also called Dr. Seiford, who told her to tell me that Zeak would never be given that drug again. Then the vet told me that she was waiving her fee in honor of Zeak's service as a therapy dog. I told her that he wasn't the same status as a seeing-eye dog, and that I certainly would never expect that. She said that she knew that, but she wanted to do it. I thanked her for her kindness. And this was not the only time that vets waived their fee for The Zeakie Dog.

Because, by definition, remission means there is no sign of illness, there was no reason Zeakie could not work. And since he loved his job, he had been back on duty for a few weeks. The extra work of his regimens was taking a toll on me, though, and I knew managing my own condition meant not overdoing. So we had to go to smaller facilities, because I couldn't handle all the walking at the bigger ones. The same was true of my work with Lakota. It wasn't the dog-—it was me. The conventional treatment was easy for me. It was the holistic regimen that was challenging me. But I was determined to do everything I possibly could for The Zeakie Dog.

And as I did, it was as if he knew it was hard for me. He was so cooperative that it was remarkable. He and I became closer than ever—we could communicate so well and easily. And, as hard as it must have been for him with all he was going through, he still took care of me. One night I was sitting, watching TV, half asleep, when Zeakie got up and started bowing in front of me, and speaking Zeakinese, frantically. Then he stared into my eyes, and used his long nose to point, and direct my gaze to the floor by the fireplace. There on the carpet was the biggest spider I have ever seen. I called Bill, because we couldn't let this thing escape, especially if it was poisonous. I kept my eye on it while he got the vacuum, and using the long tube—hoping the spider would fit up it—vacuumed it up, and got it out of the house. I walked barefoot right where that spider had been, all the time. My boy still had my back!

On a Sunday morning, my grandson, Shy, Lakota, and Zeakie and I started walking down the lower trail to the dam. We were about to unleash the dogs when all three stopped. A moment later, a big black bear emerged from the woods just a little ways down the trail, maybe thirty or forty feet. The dogs got out in front of us and went into major defensive mode, barking—no, roaring—and lunging to the point we had to wrap the leashes around trees to hold them back. Thankfully, the bear thought better of messing with the three of them and took off. Two weeks before this, a black Lab had been killed by a bear in our town. We had no doubt that our dogs would have gone down to protect us, even The Zeakie Dog, who was fighting a big enough battle of his own.

Thanksgiving was just around the corner. Our tradition was to spend it with friends—my kids went to my daughter-in-law's family. This year the feast was at our house, and I made a huge turkey, because my dogs l-o-v-e-d turkey! Everyone overate, and the dogs were no exception. We then played Trivial Pursuit, while the dogs slept in front of the fire. Because of the gift of cancer, I noticed—smelled, tasted, touched, and savored—every precious day, minute, and second of these wonderful days. I can't say there weren't moments when fear entered my mind, like in the dream I had about the monster on the lake. But I smashed fear down with my paddle. And like the monster, it disappeared under the surface of the water…for now.

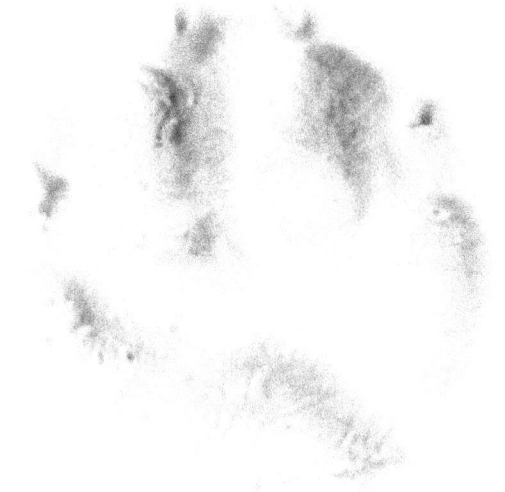

Cooper and Ice in happier times—they just wanted to have fun.

CHAPTER 25

Cooper and Ice: 2010

I read once that there is a Native American tribe that believes when one member of the tribe departs this life, another enters. And so it was in 2010 for our pack. One cold, sunny December afternoon when Lakota, Zeakie, and I were out playing in the snow in the dog yard, a visitor—or actually two visitors—arrived at the gate. It was Elaine and Cooper. Cooper had all his shots, and had grown into a sturdy enough pup to meet my boys. Elaine carried him in and set him down. Lots and lots of sniffing commenced, and Cooper—a little intimidated by the sheer size of his two new acquaintances—rolled over on his back in submission.

Lakota and Zeak had satisfied their curiosity, and went back to playing in the snow. It was obvious that the puppy really wanted to go play with them, but was too frightened to join the roughhousing yet. He stood at Elaine's feet with his eyes fixed on the two big dogs who were wrestling in the snow. Then Lakota and Zeak reared up on their hind legs with their front legs pawing the air and showed their teeth to each other. This was all in good dog fun, and the puppy thought it was the coolest thing he had ever seen. So he decided to try it. There was little Cooper, all by himself, rearing up on his hind legs, showing his puppy teeth, and snapping at the air like his bigger and older counterparts. Elaine and I laughed at the adorable antics of this pup, who was so mesmerized by the two older dogs.

Elaine said that she had noticed how well behaved and nice Lakota and Zeak were, and asked if she could bring

Cooper up to play with them regularly. Unfortunately, though most of the dogs in the area got along, there were a few very unruly, ill-tempered, even dangerous dogs in our community. It only takes a small amount of time to train a dog, coupled with consistency from everyone in the house. It is so much more pleasurable to spend time with a respectful, well-behaved dog—I have never understood why any dog owner would not want this. Even though this was her first dog, Elaine knew that dogs were pack animals and that her puppy would imitate the behavior of his friends. (Is this not also true for humans?) So she thought it would be a great way to naturally train Cooper. I agreed, and this was the beginning of a beautiful friendship, and not just for our dogs.

Lakota and Zeak were the perfect tag team for the puppy. At our first few play dates, Cooper wouldn't even approach The Zeakie Dog. It was as though he saw him as some kind of unapproachable rock star! He would play and run around with Lakota, but just look at Zeak from afar. After a couple of weeks of this, he started to approach Zeak, then run away. This game escalated into approaching Zeak, showing his puppy teeth at him, and running away. Gradually he got bolder, and Zeak started to respond by speaking to Cooper in Zeakinese, and then chasing him, which Cooper delighted in. Zeak taught Cooper respect and gave him thrills and excitement. Lakota, with his calm, patient, gentle demeanor, gave the puppy confidence. As the months passed by, their play dates became a part of every day, and the friendship among the three deepened, and they became family.

And so it was with Elaine and me. We became very good friends, bonded by our love of our dogs. We were there for each other, to help and support one another through life's difficult times, and we too became like family.

This brings to mind one of the more delicate problems that vets have to deal with, which is similar to one that human doctors dance around: weight control. Back in primitive times, a strong food drive was necessary for survival for both humans and dogs. Now with food in abundance here, those of us with a strong food drive—I am a part of this group—are always fighting the battle of the bulge. Cooper was a hungry boy with very loving owners, and he had gotten quite good at extorting extra food from them, using his adorable smile. And he was a bench dog, so he didn't have a strong exercise drive. As time went by, he got rounder and rounder.

I was concerned about the effect this was having on his joints, and tried to broach the subject delicately. However, I sensed that his owners were taking offense, so I backed off. I figured that eventually their vet would say something. He didn't. I suggested they ask him what he thought Cooper's optimum weight was. The problem was, that when they asked their vet if Cooper was overweight, this reminded the vet all too well of his wife asking him if her new jeans made her look fat; so he chose what most husbands choose: to not tell his wife (or the pet owners standing in front of him) the truth. As a vet, it was probably for fear of losing Cooper's owners' business. As a husband, it was for fear of losing his life! Finally they visited a veterinary nutritionist, whom they were consulting about Cooper's food allergies. She put their dog's health before her wallet, and told them the truth: that their dog was more than ten pounds overweight, and needed to go on a diet.

I was relieved that the problem was being addressed, and soon Cooper had slimmed down and looked like the handsome bench dog he was. Our pack's new member was back on track to good health, and hopefully a long, happy life.

Once or twice, I have touched upon the dark side of dog ownership. Simply put, it is loss. In a perfect world, you and your dog would have the exact same life span, and all would be well. Nobody ever tells you, when you get a dog, just how bad it will be when you have to say goodbye. Perhaps it is because this relationship is the only truly unconditional love that exists here. All human forms of love have their limits. It may take extremes to break some bonds, such as maternal love. But they can—and have—been broken. No one loves you like your dog. It will love you and accept you on any terms. Dogs are so much more pure than we are, in that even if their owner/guardian does not meet their needs, they will still love him/her. They don't ask for anything in return, except your love. They don't care if you: share their opinions, look a particular way, do what they want you to, go where they want you to, or say what they want you to. They just want to love and be loved. Do not ever underestimate the positive effect that has on your life while they are with you, and the devastation it brings when it is no longer there.

The yellow Labrador with the heart problem that Ice loved so dearly passed on. He was eleven years old. Ice was fifteen—the dog equivalent of a human who is over a hundred. We all felt that one of the reasons she had been hanging in there so long was that she didn't want to leave her sweetheart.

After she lost him, Ice began to go downhill. Erin was now doing serious, extreme dog care. If she hadn't been retired, she wouldn't have been able to give Ice the care she needed. But she was, and so she did: never leaving her, unless her husband John was home to stay with her, staying up with her at night when she needed to go out or to be cleaned up from not being able to get out in time, cooking for her, lifting the dog in and out of the car, making trips to the vet for treatments for her physical issues, and bringing her for play dates with her dog friends, to keep her spirits up. Her love for and dedication to her dog were something rare and noble. And John backed her up because he loved Ice too.

There are people who think that an animal is somehow less worthy of this kind of love and care than a human being. It is my belief that they are missing the point. It matters not to whom we give our love, but rather that we give it. It matters not who receives our energy and work and time, but that we are willing to sacrifice those things for love. I believe that the worth and progress of our souls lies in our willingness to do these things for the ones we love, whoever and whatever they may be.

Even with all the love, care, and work in the world, Ice left us on December 2 of 2010—just a little over a month from her sixteenth birthday—a very long life for a dog. When we lose someone or some living thing that we love that deeply, the very love that gives us such joy when we are with the beloved, turns on us and wounds us, so mortally sometimes that we wonder if we will ever recover. And even after the terrible, seemingly endless pain and grieving, we still turn around and love again; because we are so brave. And that is one of the most redeeming characteristics of the human species.

Ice—a sweet and affectionate, but fiercely protective little Australian Shepherd, whose markings resembled war paint! Even with all the love, care, and work in the world, Ice left us in December of 2010.

CHAPTER 26

The Fireplace: After November 13, 2011

It is a very sorrowful holiday season for us this year. A few weeks before Christmas, I made myself put a tree up and made myself decorate it, because I needed to keep things in some kind of holiday spirit, to lift my mood, and to keep things as cheerful as possible for Lakota, my family, and me. But I miss Zeak terribly, and I can't even do a good job of faking seasonal enthusiasm.

It is a Friday evening a few days before Christmas. Bill is upstairs, and Lakota and I are in the living room. Lakota has been asleep on the floor by me, when something startles him and wakes him up. He has "that" look he gets only when he senses Zeak's presence: shock, and intense interest on his face. His eyes are open, bulging in awe. He sees something in the area of the fireplace and the Christmas tree next to it. His head moves around as his eyes follow it, but he stays next to me. He sniffs the air, trying to pick up a scent to explain what he sees. Then he goes over to the Christmas tree and starts sniffing the air around it. I see nothing but Lakota reacting to what he is seeing. Then he comes back to me and his eyes follow something moving from the tree, across to the other side of the fireplace.

Our fireplace is a gas fireplace, with a large mechanical switch that takes a good firm push to turn it on and off, and snaps loudly into one or the other position. There is no middle position that it can get hung up on. We are about five feet away from the fireplace. No one—nothing—is near the switch. There have been no children here. The switch is too high for Lakota to bump, and we never walk on the hearth because it's too close to the hot glass on the front of the fireplace. No one has been here all day but Lakota and me; and no one here has used the fireplace or touched the switch. So I am utterly amazed when the fireplace turns itself on. It has never done this before or since. Lakota's reaction to something unseen, coupled with the fireplace turning itself on…Merry Christmas, Zeakie!

The winter of 2011 was kind to us—it gave us lots of fluffy, white snow for the dogs to play in.

CHAPTER 27

The Last Winter: Winter of 2011

Ice's passing made for a subdued Christmas for what was left of the pack. We had a Christmas party for the dogs as we usually did, but Erin and John just stopped by briefly. We missed Ice, and it cast a shadow on the festivities to know that our senior dog was no longer with us, and her owners were grieving. But we also knew that we had to make this the best Christmas ever for Zeakie. For while it was unspoken, we did not know if he would ever have another one.

So I spent a lot of money that we didn't have on dog toys. I wrapped them in white tissue paper, since the dogs loved to unwrap their own gifts, and put them under the tree. Christmas morning the dogs each had a huge pile of toys to unwrap. They loved it! They made the biggest mess ever in our living room. It looked as if it had snowed inside. There was ripped-up white tissue and toy fluff everywhere. I had some disturbing, frightening thoughts along the lines of, "We will never do this again" intrude on my fun. I kept trying to squash them, but they kept coming back. I finally stopped them by deciding I would not allow these thoughts because Zeak would sense them, and it would keep us from enjoying this time together.

I roasted a big turkey for Christmas Eve, so that for days, the dogs could enjoy leftovers with us. We went to my son and daughter-in-law's for Christmas with the dogs. And the dogs enjoyed sharing the bounty of a Christmas dinner that we splurged on: a whole grilled filet mignon. Lakota and Zeak and Shy each had some with their Christmas Dinner.

In consideration of our vet bills, we had made a group decision to forgo spending money on gifts that we didn't need, and just give gifts to our grandson and the dogs, and invest a great feast instead.

January came, and we marked Lakota's seventh birthday, and Zeakie's fifth, with a dog cake and a gathering. Again, we tried to make it as fun and special as we could, even though it was a hard time because we knew Erin and John were grieving, and the pack had lost two dogs. As the winter passed, Erin found life without a dog to not be a life well-lived, and she and John adopted a puppy. He was beautiful: a Siberian Husky with snow-white hair with grey and black shading. They named him Tundra, and his introduction to the pack was just the shot in the arm we all needed.

After they had him a few weeks, they asked Donna to come and evaluate the puppy, who was quite a change from Ice. After checking him out, Donna told them that this dog was "no Ice," and that they were going to have to be firm and very strong leaders, to keep him in line. She also recommended play dates with Lakota and Zeak to help balance him.

They took what she said and ran with it. Tundra was very lucky that two very experienced dog owners had adopted him, and he found himself in doggy boot camp at home! They did a great job with him, and not only did he shape up, but I think it was a good thing that he was so different from Ice. The fact that they had to keep "on" him gave them a respite and a distraction from the sadness, for at least some of the time; and soon he was able to be off-leashed with the rest of the pack. And it was like old times, again to have Erin rejoining us for walks.

I noticed how the relationship between her husband John and The Zeakie Dog had grown. They had bonded very quickly when Zeakie was a young pup. John loved Zeakie's vibrant personality, and rather surprising sense of humor. And he played with him like two dogs would play, play bowing and chasing him. This game went on right till the end, with John pulling his sweatshirt hood over his head, and chasing Zeak around—sometimes crawling on his knees! It was quite a sight and comic relief for all of us.

People who have never had a close relationship with an animal have no way of gauging, or understanding, how deep the love between a human and an animal can be. It is something that truly must be experienced to be understood. And even among animal lovers, there are great variations in the depth of those relationships, ranging from animals simply being livestock, to members of the family and then some.

One afternoon I had to make a trip to our local pet-supply store for some things. I decided to bring the dogs with me. When we walked in the door, a very tall man asked if I needed any help. I told him what I was looking for, and he and I walked around collecting the items. At some point he asked me if he could give the dogs a treat, and I told him that I would prefer he didn't, because my one dog could not have any commercially prepared food because he was battling cancer. Try as I might, I just couldn't deliver that line without tearing up.

He looked at me and said, "He's 'The One,' isn't he?" I asked him what he meant. He told me that he was a trainer of search and rescue dogs, and had owned numerous dogs of his own. Last year he was lifting his German Shepherd into the back of his truck, when the dog screamed. He rushed it to the vet, where he got the news that the dog had terminal pancreatic cancer, and it needed to be put down. With his eyes filling, he looked at me and said, "Of all the dogs I have had, that dog was 'The One'—the dog you have a special connection with that surpasses all others. It's like you know each other's thoughts. You have the deepest bond."

I thought about it and said, "Yes. I love both my dogs, and I loved all my past dogs—but this one IS different. Everything is so easy with him. It's like the human/dog equivalent of soulmates. We are so much alike—we think alike, we feel similar ways about a lot of things, and we have similar anxieties and comforts. We even find a lot of the same things funny. I can tell this by his actions, expressions, and body language. He's like me, with four legs and fur. So little training was needed. He just knows what I want, and he does it. There is a special connection between us that can't be denied, and it's been this way right from the start."

I paid for my purchases, put the dogs in the SUV, and drove home thinking about the conversation. It was the first time I had actually acknowledged to myself how different things were between The Zeakie Dog and me, than they have ever been with any other dog, even Santana. And yes, Zeak was "The One."

On the home front, Elaine had been bringing Cooper up for daily play dates. And as all puppies do, Cooper entered his "bratty" stage. One day we were all out in the dog yard, and Cooper stole my glove. Elaine firmly told him to "drop," but he just took off at top speed. This disrespect for me was more than The Zeakie Dog could take. No one said a word to Zeak. He just saw the situation and went into action. He ran Cooper down so fast he didn't know what hit him. Then with a look, he made him drop the glove, picked it up, ran it back to me, and dropped it at my feet! I was deeply touched, and amazed by his intelligence. You see things like this in movies, but rarely do you get to experience them in real life. I kneeled down, put my arms around his neck, and hugged him and thanked him.

Unfortunately, Cooper thought this was all great fun. For the rest of the winter, he kept stealing gloves, hats, toys—anything he could latch on to, and Zeak would get it back. Eventually Lakota started helping Zeak and they would tag-team the puppy, to retrieve whatever it was that he had stolen. Elaine and I marveled at this: The dogs were taking care of things for us…while we consumed way too much coffee!

Another example of Zeak watching my back happened one morning when I was doing laundry in the basement. I had bent over to pick up a sock, and when I stood up, I smashed my head on the saw table—so hard that I screamed. Zeakie always had trouble going down our steep cellar stairs and was afraid of them, but when he heard me from outside he ran down them fearlessly, at top speed. He rushed over to me and started giving me rapid-fire kisses, and was obviously very concerned. When I stood up and told him I was OK, he smiled at me and did a Zeakie Dance.

And so, the winter of 2011 was kind to us. It gave us lots of fluffy white snow for the dogs to play in. The Zeakie Dog ran through deep snow and even drifts with such force and strength, that it sent showers of white powder flying out sideways from his body. He ate enthusiastically, played enthusiastically, and loved his friends and his brother and us.

He went for his chemo treatments and did not have any problems at all, for the entire winter. I thanked God and I thanked Dr. Seiford, who was working miracles with him on every visit. He visited the sick, and the lonely, and even the dying; and lifted them up, and even made them smile. And he gave me more love and affection than anyone, or anything, has ever given me for all the years I have been on this earth.

Tundra did not give Zeak the respect that all of the other dogs did. So The Zeakie Dog invested a lot of time and energy in fixing that. And then, the play took a different turn, and became affectionate.

CHAPTER 28

The Last Spring: Spring of 2011

Winter fought for all it was worth, but Spring won out. Gradually, the snows melted and things started getting greener and waking up. We were enjoying our lightened load as we hiked without so much gear to keep us warm. Everyone had enough of cold and shoveling snow—everyone except me. I did not want to see winter end because that meant time…time that was moving forward, time that I desperately wanted to stand still.

However, The Zeakie Dog was feeling so well that I was beginning to feel hopeful. Our frequent trips to Animals First were building a bond between Dr. Seiford, her techs, and me. It was like we were all fighting a war against a common enemy. I could not possibly express enough gratitude to them. And The Zeakie Dog was winning their affection, just the way he had with all of us.

I wanted to do something for the people who were caring for my dog—and also for other people who loved their dogs and had to face a diagnosis like we had. I decided to make a video to show the incredible quality of life that our dog was experiencing while undergoing chemo treatment. It would have made it so much easier for me to make the decision in favor of chemo, if I had seen something like that. I remembered well how much the woman with the Great Pyrenees had helped me. So I began shooting footage of Zeak's romps with his friends, his spectacular leaping catches of the Frisbee and ball, and his tearing into the lake and sending a wall of water spraying in every direction. Zeakie was doing so well that I was beginning to wonder if my prayers for a miracle were going to be realized. I was thinking about that one night when I just felt like lying on my bed with the dogs. Zeakie jumped up and snuggled next to me, and then rolled over on his back and asked for a belly rub. I rubbed his belly and massaged his legs and he smiled the biggest grin. And then that voice in me that I had been able to silence for a while said, "Savor this moment—savor it, because it will not last—remember everything about it."

Zeakie and Tundra had been evolving in their relationship. At first, Zeak seemed to think the new puppy was an incredible pest! Tundra did not give Zeak the respect that all of the other dogs did. So, The Zeakie Dog invested a lot of time and energy in fixing that. There were many romps, with Zeak correcting the pup, and trying to get him to give him his due as the pack leader. And then, the play took a different turn, and became affectionate. The two of them would lie down and start mouthing and "talking" to each other. And gradually, the Zeakinese and the Tundra sounds began to take on an almost musical quality. None of us had ever seen or heard two dogs play quite like this before. It was a beautiful and haunting sound—a little like wolves make when they are all howling at once, but quieter and gentler.

It was June 14—a Tuesday—and Lakota, Zeakie, and I headed for Animals First for Zeakie's chemo treatment. Zeakie's and my favorite tech, Catherine, came out to take him in. The usual procedure was that they would check his blood, and then Dr. Seiford would examine him, and come out and tell me how he was doing. Today was no different—except the usual smile on Dr. Seiford's face looked different. I got up to greet her with the usual hug, and then we sat down to talk. She looked me square in the eye, and slowly said, "Zeak may be coming out of remission." She told me that it could be allergies, or fighting off an infection, but she had felt "something" in his lymph nodes.

I assured her that he was acting like he was in the peak of health; he hadn't slowed down a bit. He was eating enthusiastically, playing with his friends, jumping over fallen trees, and tearing through the woods like a deer. That he couldn't possibly be....

She said, "I know…but these hands…." She looked down at her hands and then at me. And without another word, I understood that those hands had a gift. I understood that she was not the renowned veterinary oncologist she was simply because of her extensive studies. She was the whole package. She had the instinct, the intuition, and the gifted hands of a master. And those hands had felt something they did not want to feel—something she didn't want to have to tell me about, but had to.

She told me we would give him his chemo, and hope she was wrong; and she wanted to see him again in two weeks. I had been keeping my composure till now, but finally the dam broke, and the tears just poured out of my eyes. She took me into an examining room and hugged me, while I had the good cry I so desperately needed. Then she told me to stay in there as long as I needed to, and said that she would see me in two weeks.

When I had composed myself, I went to the front desk to pay my bill. The young woman at the desk was a big fan of The Zeakie Dog, and she had been there during his first illness. Her name was Penny, and she was one of those people who had fallen in love with The Zeakie Dog instantly. When I told her what Dr. Seiford said, she started to cry. She came out from behind the desk and kneeled down and put her arms around Zeakie. He gave her a gazillion rapid-fire kisses and made her laugh; and she said that she would be praying for him. I thanked her, because I knew she really meant it. Then I drove home, trying desperately to smash down the fear rising in me.

*How would I know when it was time to let Zeakie go?
And how could I possibly do that?*

CHAPTER 29

The Last Summer: 2011

From the moment that Zeakie had been diagnosed, I had spent all the time I could educating myself about canine lymphoma. As a result, I knew way more than I wanted to about the subject. I needed that knowledge to give my dog the best care. I hit the books, scoured the internet, and devoured every detail of what Dr. Seiford said, hoping it would make a difference.

The next two weeks flew by with Zeakie feeling great and enjoying life. Then it was time for his appointment. I had butterflies in my stomach all the way over. The tech came out and asked how Zeak was doing. I told her, and then she took him in the back. A few minutes later, Dr. Seiford came out and sat down by me. She looked me in the eye, and slowly told me that Zeak was now out of remission. I focused on the information she was giving to suppress the wave of nausea that washed over me. She said we would now start rescue protocol, and she gave me a sheet of paper with information on the different treatments. When she said the words "rescue protocol," I flashed back to something I had read, about how rescue protocol is not as effective as the original protocol, but it's all we have and it's better than nothing.

The sheet with the protocols gave their odds of producing a remission and the kinds of, and likelihood of, various side effects. And then I saw that a possible side effect of the last protocol was…death. I immediately noticed that the odds of remission were lower and the chances of side effects greater than in the original protocol. She decided to use these treatments a bit out of order, and explained why she thought it was best for him to do it that way. He would be given nausea meds to keep him from feeling sick.

So we shifted gears, didn't miss a beat, and moved forward. I was now fighting the fear trying to take me over, because I didn't want Zeak to pick up on it. We had been so successful at beating down the beast for so long that I had allowed myself to let my guard down. At this point, I remembered a Chinese proverb I had read once: "Beware the tail of the dragon." Even after the dragon appeared to be dead, the tail could rise up and get you.

When I got home, I called Erin and Elaine to deliver the upsetting news that Zeakie was now out of remission. A few hours later, as I was preparing dinner, I got a call from Erin. She told me she had told John about Zeak and that he was upset, and felt he had to see Zeakie. She had tried to stop him, because she didn't know if we were up to a visit, but he was on his way over. I went out and unlocked the back gate, and decided to let him have his visit with Zeakie alone, because I knew John needed it. And I would just continue what I was doing in the house.

As soon as John arrived, Zeak went out the dog door to bark at the visitor. I kept Lakota in with me. As I worked, I could see out the window. John opened the gate and went into the dog yard. He got down on the ground and hugged The Zeakie Dog. Then they started playing. They chased each other, rolled around in the grass and dirt with each other, and generally played like two dogs, except one of them wasn't a dog! I let it go on for quite a while, but then I became concerned that Zeak might be overdoing it. So I went out and told John he could stay as long as he wished, but requested that they have a calm, quiet visit now. I explained that Zeak had just received a new protocol, and his body needed rest. We both avoided making eye contact, because it would have opened the flood of emotions that we were both holding back, trying to deal with this frightening development. He stayed a while longer, then left.

It was touching to see how much The Zeakie Dog meant to John. He and Erin were still mourning Ice, and now they had to hear this bad news. I had noticed, over the years, that The Zeakie Dog had a profound effect on certain people. I was not the only one who fell in "love at first sight" with him. Everywhere we went, it was like he was invisible to some people, while others were overwhelmed by him. They would come over and ask about him. Many would start to pet him, and kneel down to be at eye level. Several pet owners at Animals First had done that—one teenage girl hugging him and saying over and over how beautiful he was.

Zeakie got through three days on the new protocol, and then something happened: on the fourth morning, he looked as though he was going to refuse breakfast. Never in Zeak's life had he refused food, or even looked like he was going to. The timing suggested it was a reaction to the chemo. The next three mornings the same thing happened; he looked like he was going to walk away from his food, but then ate it all. It would appear he was nauseous, but once he started eating, the nausea went away. For the rest of the three weeks, till we were to see Dr. Seiford again, he was fine.

On Thursday morning of the third week from his last treatment, we went back to Animals First. When Dr. Seiford came out, the news was not good. No progress; that was the end of that protocol. I could tell she was disappointed that it hadn't worked. Now we would try the biggest gun of all the rescue protocols: MOPP. One of the "P"s stood for prednisone. Now he would be getting it to manage the side effects of the other powerful drugs he was getting. This was our best shot at getting a second remission. The tail of the dragon/snake was rising and getting stronger and more resistant to the drugs.

I asked Dr. Seiford to please teach me how to find and feel Zeakie's lymph nodes. I wanted to learn this so I could check them at home every day, and report any big changes to her. She agreed, so I learned. And then she did something that spoke to the trust that had developed between us: She gave me her cell phone number. I would never have asked for it. It went unspoken that it would only be used in the direst emergency. I knew that the proper thing to do if there was a problem was to bring Zeak in and let the emergency vet determine if Dr. Seiford needed to be called; then he or she would call her. I would never use it unless…why would I use it? I didn't know, but she must have had a reason. I thanked her, and told her I would never intrude on her private time, unless it was totally necessary. And as I drove home I started to think about a thing I never wanted to even imagine, but had to: How would I know if, and when, it was time to let Zeakie go, and how could I possibly do that?

*At this point, I remembered a Chinese proverb I had read once: "Beware the tail of the dragon."
Just as I had started to relax, trust that things were going well, and feel safe—it struck us.*

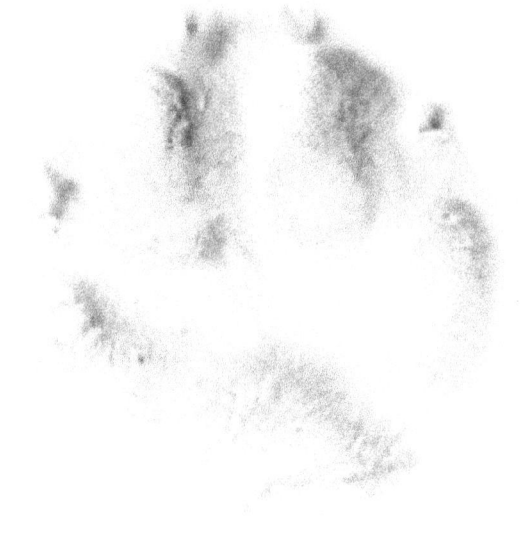

CHAPTER 30

A Dog in Macy's?: After November 13, 2011

It has been seven months now. I am in Macy's looking for some items in the ladies' clothing department. It is a weekday afternoon, and this section of the ladies' sportswear department is totally empty except for me. I am temporarily distracted from the unending ache in my heart, looking at a rack of knit tops, when I feel a very firm pressure on the side of my right calf. Something very warm, furry, and heavy is leaning on my bare lower leg. It is pressing so firmly that there is no question something is there. I look down to see—nothing. There is not even a sweater, a coat, or a rack nearby that could have caused this. Nothing is in my hands. My purse is hanging on my left shoulder, and could not possibly have been anywhere near my lower right leg.

Macy's?! The Zeakie Dog is with me in Macy's?! Well, I guess he can now do what he always wished he could do—come with me anywhere and anytime he wants! I am delighted by this visit. I am more accepting now that he can do this. I wish I could have some say in these visits, so that when I am aching for him I could get one, but I am thrilled and delighted to have one whenever I can. Tears of joy run down my face. I am a mess, so I go into a dressing room to do some damage control on my eye makeup, all the while thinking, "Macy's! What next?"

When I arrive home, I take Lakota out for afternoon play, and then make dinner. Bill gets home and we sit down to eat. I tell him what happened in Macy's. I am half expecting Bill the skeptic—Bill the scientist—to tell me I am imagining things. But instead, he tells me he felt something brush against his leg, under the table at dinner, a few nights ago. It wasn't Lakota—he could see him lying by me, where he always did. He definitely felt something. But there was nothing there. He has been wondering if it was Zeak.

Our lovely bubble had burst: MOPP, the biggest gun in the arsenal, and our best hope... had failed.

CHAPTER 31

MOPP: July & Early August 2011

The day after Dr. Seiford administered the MOPP protocol, Zeakie woke up weak and exhausted. He went out, came in, ate his breakfast, and went to sleep in the dining room. We took our walk a couple of hours later, but he was tired. However, sometime in the afternoon, the prednisone kicked in, and so did The Zeakie Dog! Now I had this playful, smiling dog who was extremely hungry. I was thrilled! I gave him dinner and several snacks. He gave me a gazillion rapid-fire kisses and numerous Zeakie Dances. The next day I checked his lymph nodes, and was elated to find them getting mushy. That had to mean they were going down. It was looking like the MOPP protocol was making real progress.

Meanwhile, Zeak was ravenous. He kept going into the kitchen, speaking profuse Zeakinese, and smiling at me. He wanted more food, and I could swear, from his body language, he was actually embarrassed, because he knew he had just eaten. Before we walked, I filled him up, as best I could, with cooked string beans in organic chicken broth. I didn't want him eating stuff off the ground in the woods because he was so hungry.

One morning, as we walked up the trail to the lake, Zeakie came running over to me frantically shaking his paw at me. I looked at the top of his paw and there was a tick on it. This dog was so smart it was mind-boggling! He had seen me remove a few ticks from him that had gotten past the control meds over the years. He had remembered that they were undesirable and had to be pulled out. Now he was showing me when he got a tick on him! I had never had a dog do that, and never heard of a dog doing that. A few days later, he came to me again, this time to show me a tick on top of his long nose. The ticks were really abundant now, and the controls were not working perfectly, so we were all removing some from our dogs. But to everyone's amazement, The Zeakie Dog was actually finding them when they got on him, and pointing them out to me, so I could remove them before they embedded!

Zeak had a great week. He was hungry all the time, gained weight, was full of energy, and even playing Frisbee again. On Saturday we walked with Erin and John and Tundra. Zeak started playing with Tundra, chasing him all around the meadow. It was a major romp! We were all marveling that this dog was out of remission, yet still so full of energy and power. It went on for so long that we decided to stop it, fearful that Zeakie was overdoing it. One week later we had to go for another treatment. Dr. Seiford checked his nodes and said they were fifty percent smaller.

Then I did something I had to do. I asked her the question that had been relentlessly popping up in my mind—how would I know when it was time to let Zeakie go? Were there guidelines? She told me when he couldn't eat most of the time, and was too weak to get up and greet people; then the quality of life is not there. I filed that away in my brain—I knew I would remember that. That was straightforward. That was clear. That would make the decision, one I could make based on definite markers, so I couldn't screw it up. I didn't want to make it one day too soon, and miss even one day with him. I didn't want to make it one day too late, and cause him to suffer. The next morning he slept all morning, just like he did after his last treatment—then he was fine.

That Saturday, we had a dog party to mark the summer dog birthdays—Cooper, Tundra, Molly, and Shy—and to celebrate Zeak's one-year survival. We were able to celebrate because we knew there was hope: hope for another long remission. It was a wonderful, joyful day for all of us. Donna came with four of her dogs, and I don't know who had more fun, the dogs or us. Cooper was now attending our parties, and he took a real liking to Baxter, the little blind dog that Donna had rescued. He hung out with Baxter while the dogs played outside. It was as though Baxter had his own guide dog!

Zeakie felt great and had a wonderful time playing with his friends, both canine and human, and enjoying dog cake with no sugar or honey added. I had read that sugar is food for cancer cells, so we were being very careful about that. The dog bakery made the cake to our specifications, and the dogs seemed to love the cake, anyway.

The next week, I noticed a little dip in Zeakie's energy level. He had stopped playing Frisbee. I was checking his nodes daily, and it was a good thing I had learned to do it, because on Wednesday I was horrified to find them substantially larger. I called Animals First and Dr. Seiford got on the phone. When I told her how big his nodes were, she told me to come in at eight a.m. the next morning. Our lovely bubble had burst: MOPP—the biggest gun in the arsenal and our best hope—had failed.

*Our lake community was cut off by a storm—
we were trapped!*

CHAPTER 32

Hurricane Irene and Other Disasters: August 2011

Early the next morning we arrived at Animals First. Dr. Seiford examined Zeakie and came out to talk. We hugged and sat down. She told me that the next best chance for The Zeakie Dog was a protocol involving a six-hour IV drip. I had a hard time with this. I didn't want Zeakie in a cage for six hours—he had enough of that when he was a puppy. I also didn't want him away from home and me for that long; I felt it would be too stressful for him. She told me that we still had a good chance for a remission. I told her that I would OK the IV, provided that they gave Zeakie sedation—enough that he didn't care where he was. She agreed to do it.

Catherine came out for him. She told me not to worry, that they weren't super busy today, and she would spend any time she had free with Zeakie. I noticed she had on a very light vanilla fragrance. Zeakie was not thrilled when she led him to the door to the back rooms, but he followed obediently.

I couldn't leave. I had brought some work with me—a dog portrait I was working on for someone—so I stayed and worked and prayed. It was around 2:30 when they brought The Zeakie Dog out. I could tell they had sedated him because he was perfectly delighted to be there, and in no hurry to leave. He usually wanted out, now! But today he was just "hanging out" while Catherine and I talked. She said he had slept through most of his treatment, and she had spent quite a bit of time sitting in front of his cage, with the door open and his head on her lap.

When I helped Zeak into the car, I noticed a slight scent of vanilla on his fur. Catherine had been true to her word. These were such good people. They genuinely cared for The Zeakie Dog, and were going all out to save him and keep him comfortable. I drove home hopeful, on one of the uphill sides of the roller coaster the last few weeks had been. As soon as we got home, The Zeakie Dog wanted FOOD—NOW!

This protocol could produce some nausea, so Zeakie was now on two nausea meds, one of which made him pant a lot. At this point, I was once again administering over sixty meds and supplements to Zeak daily. He was no longer on prednisone with this protocol. The next day, he ran around in the woods with Lakota and another dog. A young, wild, large, year-old Labradoodle pup. Zeak seemed to be having fun, but then dropped down to rest, exhausted. After he rested, he walked home normally.

The next three days Zeakie did not feel well or want to eat in the morning, but he made up for it in the afternoon. On the fourth day, he perked up and brought me the Frisbee and wanted to play. And so it went for the next two weeks. He felt better, ate, played, and had more energy. There was just one problem: The nodes were not going down. They were not going up, either. We were just maintaining—waiting for the next IV treatment. We needed that treatment badly because we were just holding our own. It was scheduled for Thursday, September 1.

But Mother Nature had other plans. A few days before Zeakie's IV chemo was to be administered, Hurricane Irene tore through New Jersey, and when she left, much of our state was under water, including Animals First. The building itself was up high enough to be safe, but nobody could get in or out. Firemen had evacuated vets, techs, and animals—in boats. A couple of animals that were too critical to be moved stayed in the building with a dedicated vet who volunteered to stay with them, and care for them. The rest were moved to another facility.

Our lake community was cut off. We were trapped. Roads were impassable, covered with branches and downed trees. There was no power. No phone service except for cell phones. Zeakie was due for chemo, and we couldn't even get out of our lake community. And even if we could, nobody was getting into, or out of, Animals First.

Fortunately, storm-wise, we were well prepared. We had bought a generator after Hurricane Floyd, years earlier. So had many of our neighbors—in fact, everyone on our street had one. People who had them were sharing lines with neighbors who didn't, to keep their freezers cold. We ran our generator three times a day; the rest of the time we did without it to conserve gas, since there was no way to get more. We had to keep the dog food freezer and our other freezer cold, but we had some room in them, so we had suggested Elaine and Allie bring up all of their perishables. We also charged all of our cell phones while the generator was running. We had two battery-operated lanterns, a gas range, and a gas fireplace, which we needed because it was quite cold at night. So we were fine—except we couldn't get the treatment Zeakie needed to stay alive, and I was frightened—terrified for him.

The day after Zeakie missed his chemo, his nodes were noticeable larger. I called the facility where the dogs who had been evacuated were taken, and I was able to get one of the techs from Animals First. I explained our predicament. The tech told me that Dr. Seiford was working on it—trying to find another facility where the chemo could be given. The problem was that chemo had to be administered in a specially certified building, to prevent contamination in just such situations as we were experiencing now. As the tech went on, I was beginning to panic. Not only could I not get chemo for Zeak, but I couldn't get to a vet, period. Once a dog is out of remission, serious situations can arise quickly. If he was suffering, we couldn't even get help to euthanize him. Again, I squashed down the panic and jammed it with positive thoughts to calm myself. There was nothing else I could do.

Chainsaws ripped all around us from sunrise to sunset every day. On the fifth day, our roads were finally cleared and opened. Then I got a call from Catherine to tell me that Animals First had commandeered a big truck, and the waters had receded enough to get the staff in, with the truck. Dr. Seiford and her techs were going to meet us early in the morning and work all day, to treat all of the dogs who needed chemo. They told me where to park, and the truck would meet us, to bring us in.

We were up before dawn, because with many of the roads under water, it could take a while to get there. Friends who had been in the area recently helped me route our way, telling me which roads were open and which were flooded out; and get there, we did. And as we got near, we found a way around the road that was still under water; and the water had receded enough around Animals First that we were able to drive into the parking lot, high and mostly dry, in our own vehicle. I said prayers of gratitude as Zeakie and I walked across the wet parking lot. As we came into the building, Dr. Seiford and Catherine came out. There were hugs all around, and Zeak was quickly ushered into the back, to start his IV…too quickly. Something was wrong. I knew they were backed up, but something was feeling different. Something was not right.

I sat there in my high rubber boots, ready to wait for all six hours. It was overcast and could rain. There was no way I was leaving The Zeakie Dog, when it could flood again. As I sat there, something was troubling me. I couldn't quite put my finger on what was wrong. On the one hand, I was so relieved that Zeak was getting his chemo. But something just felt…troubling. Everybody had been pleasant enough, so I just chalked it up to the stress of the storm, the flood, and the pressures of trying to get all the dogs—who desperately needed it—their chemo.

As I sat there pondering this and other things, one of Dr. Seiford's techs, whom I had just recently met, came to sit with me. He was a really nice and kind man, who had asked me if I wanted anything to eat, when he went out to get lunch for everybody the last time I waited for Zeakie's IV. We had chatted about Zeak, and Zeakie had really taken a liking to this tech, even giving him kisses—which had made some of the other techs a little jealous. So I thought he was just coming to chat on his break, to help me pass the time. I was totally unprepared for what he was about to tell me.

He told me he wanted to confide something, in case I had noticed that Dr. Seiford seemed a little subdued. And then he went on to tell me that a few days before the storm, Dr. Seiford felt that her beloved five-year-old Mastiff was a little "off." So she brought him in to check him over, and see if anything was wrong. What she found was her worst nightmare come true: Dr. Seiford's dog—the exact same age as Zeak—had lymph cancer. It had started on interior nodes, where it couldn't be felt. Silently, with no warning, no symptoms, the dragon/snake had attacked with such ferocity that nothing she could do, could save him…or even buy him some time. He was…gone.

Kara Seiford, the renowned, dedicated veterinary oncologist, who had given so many of our dogs the gift of a longer, better life, had just lost her own, beloved, young dog to this monstrous disease. And yet, with a broken heart, she had been looking for a way to continue treatments for the dogs in her charge, even during the flood. And she was here early this morning, saving my dog, so that I could have him to love for another day.

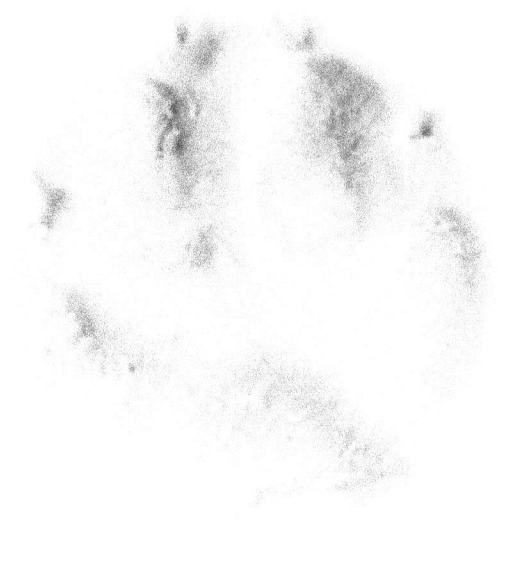

The Zeakie Dog being quite a character, with a highly honed sense of humor, wanted to cheer up his buddy.

CHAPTER 33

The Practical Joker: After November 13, 2011

It is a Friday night (once again—Zeakie seems to like to visit on Fridays), and Lakota and I are in bed. He is recuperating from a fairly minor surgical procedure. The surgery was done to remove a non-cancerous tumor that was encroaching on a muscle, and has left him feeling not-so-great, from anesthesia and a large incision. He is sleeping next to me and I am reading. All at once he wakes up and twists around—even though I suspect that is uncomfortable—to stare in shock and awe at the invisible spot. Then his eyes slowly and smoothly follow something around the room, till they come to rest...on top of my head! For several minutes he stares above my head, looking like his eyes are going to pop out of his own head. He looks almost as if he is about to panic. Then, just as suddenly, he lies back down and goes back to sleep.

From Lakota's reaction, I slowly realize what I think has happened: The Zeakie Dog, being quite a character, with a highly honed sense of humor, wanted to cheer up his buddy. So he did what always got a huge laugh, when he did it in his life here. Only this time, he sat on my *head!*

It was a memory I will always cherish, because it was the last time we were ever able to walk around the lake together.

CHAPTER 34

The Last Autumn: October 2011

As we drove home from the IV chemo, I was very upset. If anyone in the whole world deserved a long life for her dog, it was Dr. Seiford. It was so cruel and so unfair—just one more case of bad things happening to good people. It was also frightening. I guess I had been thinking of her as a worker of miracles, as unfair and unrealistic as that might seem. I thought that because it comforted me. It allowed me to sustain a flow of positive thoughts—if I prayed enough, and had the very best medical care and nutrition for Zeakie, all would be fine. It allowed me to underestimate our adversary. That was so over.

This time Zeak had less nausea from the IV chemo. However, he was refusing to eat one of his favorite things. In order to get Zeak to eat some of the supplements he was getting from the holistic vet, I was boring holes in pieces of preservative-free, organic hot dogs. (Yes—$$$$$!) I would stuff the capsules in them, and he would enjoy getting his supplements. Now Zeak was refusing them. It was as if they tasted bad to him. I tried them myself and they were fine.

A few days later he started eating them again. He had three good weeks. It was gorgeous weather, and the autumn colors were breathtaking. Zeak was feeling so well, that one beautiful day, Elaine and I decided to walk all the way around the lake with the three dogs. The hike was a little over two miles, and the dogs loved it. It was a memory I will always cherish, because it was the last time we were able to do that together.

I had been concerned, with the cold weather coming and Zeakie out of remission, that he might be cold. I had never found a dog jacket that would stay on when the dogs were off leash, running hard, in the woods. So I made him one, then I made Lakota one, and Cooper one, and—what the heck—I made one for Molly and Tundra and Shy too. I pictured a photo of all of the pack, in the snow, with their red paw print coats on, on our Christmas card.

Well, I didn't have to wait long. On October 29 of 2011, we were pounded with an incredible, early snowstorm. Leaves were still on the trees, and with the additional weight of a lot of heavy snow, trees were down everywhere, once again. The governor declared a state of emergency, we were without power for days and…I got pictures of Zeakie and his friends in their red paw print coats. I didn't know it, but it would be the last time he ever wore it.

But I was not completely avoiding what lay ahead. Something in me had been rising—something that was telling me I had to make arrangements, in case things went south fast. I needed to get this done, so I could forget it and think positively, so I got some names and called three different vets who did home euthanasia, and made arrangements, in case I needed them. With three, I would have plenty of backup. I asked around, and got references for all three, to be sure they were both competent and compassionate.

I was determined that I would let Zeakie go, before I would let him suffer. I put the three vets' names on the refrigerator, in case I needed them. I wanted him to have a peaceful, loving goodbye, at home—with the people and dogs who loved him around him. I even had relaxing music ready—calming reiki music that Zeak had good memories of. I had played this music when I hired the certified animal massage therapist and rehabilitationist after his first serious illness. He loved his massages and his therapist. It helped ease his pain and hasten his healing.

Catherine had consulted the animal behaviorist at Animals First for me, in regard to how best to handle this for all the dogs. She told me to let the dogs say goodbye, and then take them to another place. After Zeakie was put down, let them come back and sniff him IF they wanted to, so they would understand, and wouldn't search for him.

I made these arrangements in a methodical, businesslike manner—detached from thinking or feeling what they really meant, because I couldn't bear to. I had to have everything in place to keep my dog from suffering. I would do whatever it took to protect him. I had done my homework. I truly thought I had all of the bases covered.

Dr. Seiford had told me to call in after two weeks and let her know how Zeak was doing. So I placed the call, but instead of Dr. Seiford taking the call, Catherine picked up. She told me that Dr. Seiford had to have emergency abdominal surgery. She would be out for a month. Another oncologist was going to cover for her.

My heart sank, both because I was concerned for her, and because I knew there was no one who could really take her place. On the fourth week we went in for the next—and last—IV chemo. I met the new oncologist, a Dr. Rettson, and really liked him. He was very kind and caring, and from a top veterinary school. He explained that only four of these IV treatments could be given without causing damage to a dog's organs. However, after examining Zeak, Dr. Rettson declined to give him the fourth treatment. We were backsliding. His nodes were bigger. If we couldn't do better than this…it was time to change protocols.

This time we were going to try a new drug that would be given at home in pill form. We started the new med, and

Zeak tolerated it well. He was a little tired but otherwise OK for two weeks. However, his left rear leg was swelling up due to an enlarged node, and he had developed a rash on his belly. It was a Sunday, so I took him to the emergency vet on duty at Animals First. She didn't know what the rash was. She called Dr. Seiford. Dr. Seiford told her she was coming back early, and would see Zeak Tuesday morning. So Tuesday morning we headed to Animals First, to have Dr. Seiford look at Zeak. His leg was so swollen it was frightening. His belly was bright pink.

When Dr. Seiford came in, it was obvious she was in pain. She said she hoped I didn't mind if she sat down. I told her I was so glad to see her, I didn't care if she hung off the ceiling! I asked her how she was feeling. She said it was no worse at work than it was at home, so she was coming in, but trying to stay off her feet as much as she could. She examined Zeak, and told me we had to watch his lungs. They could fill with cancer cells very quickly, which meant a death by suffocation, and terrible anxiety went with that. I told her I had asthma, and I knew that feeling. I did not want Zeakie to ever have to experience that. Then I looked her in the eye and asked, "Is it time?"

"No, not yet," she said. I asked her if his leg hurt him. She said, "No—it's not painful—to him it just feels numb. Sometimes they will get a pins and needles feeling and they will let us know by biting at it. If the node bothers him we can zap it with some radiation." Then she told me that the rash on his belly was from the enlargement of the inguinal nodes. She told me we were going to initiate the last protocol. I remembered that this was the protocol with a side effect of death. She paused a minute and said, "We may be reaching the end."

I tried to keep my composure, but couldn't, so I just let the tears roll, while I listened intently. She told me we were going to give him a short burst of prednisone to get the nodes, which were huge, down. Zeak's face was all swollen and distorted from the enormous swellings. She said it was a tough call, because it would make it harder to get a remission, but it would be a quick burst and he would be too uncomfortable without it. I totally agreed with this approach.

Then, from way out of left field, she offered me the thing I needed most: hope. She told me that the first week of November—-just a week away—she was going to a worldwide veterinary conference. She told me that there would be vets there with new cancer treatments from all around the world. Then she looked me directly in the eyes and said, "If there is anything out there—anything in the world that will save him—I will bring it back."

When I see the temperature registered on the thermometer, my heart sinks. It is close to one hundred and five.

CHAPTER 35

The World Conference: the Last Protocol

My journal. November 2011:

<u>Tuesday, November 1</u>
Morning nausea passes quickly. Prednisone has helped him feel better. However, it makes him pant. His leg has gone down beautifully. Left side neck node is huge. Otherwise, Zeakie is doing well. He is hungry and eating, enjoying his friends, and enjoying his walk, walking near me off leash, and enjoying sniffing around. World conference starts in two days.

<u>Wednesday, November 2</u>
Last prednisone. Barely ate any breakfast, but from lunch on wanted to eat a lot. Playing with his friends, smiling at me, acting affectionate and like himself. World conference starts in one day.

<u>Thursday, November 3</u>
Good day, much like yesterday. Doesn't want breakfast, but has lunch, and snacks, dinner, and more snacks. We enjoy a walk in the beautiful woods. The leaves are down, and with the sun shining, everything is a warm, amber color. Later, Cooper comes over with Elaine and we all hang out in the back yard. World conference starts today!

<u>Friday, November 4</u>
Ate almost half of breakfast. After breakfast, Zeak heard something outside, and ran into the kitchen too fast. Fell hard, sliding into a cabinet with a yelp. I felt around for tender spots, but no reaction. I thought of taking him to the vet,

but he got up, shook it off, and indicated he wanted to go for his walk. So, I guess it sounded worse than it was. Still, I was upset that this had to happen to him, on top of everything else. I called Erin, and told her what happened. I was upset. It was just one more thing for this sweet dog who didn't deserve any of it.

On our walk, he seems tired from prednisone withdrawal, at least I hope that's what it's from. Concerned about his nodes—they are getting larger. They HAVE to go down! I ask Bill to go out for groceries. I am not leaving Zeak for any reason now. I cancel appointments.

<u>Saturday, November 5</u>

Zeak is panting a lot, even though he is off the prednisone. However, he is still on a nausea med, which causes dogs to pant like crazy, too. Still, his nose feels warm to me, so I take his temperature. It is almost a hundred and four degrees. Very concerned, so I put him in our SUV and take him to Animals First. The emergency vet doesn't like how his lungs sound and thinks he may have pneumonia. She prescribes antibiotics and orders a water infusion for him. This procedure is done by inserting a short, thick needle under the skin on the animal's back. Cool water is then released under the skin till it forms a large bump on the animal's back. The water gradually absorbs and hydrates the animal. I ask her to please let the tech do it in the examining room, so I can be with him. She agrees.

The tech comes in and inserts a thick needle under Zeak's skin, on his back. She also works at Dr. Weaver's, so she knows Zeakie and me. She comments on how calm, and what a good patient he is—even though I am with him. She says that's unusual—that most dogs are more nervous with their owners around. Zeakie is lying on the floor in front of me. I am watching him. He raises his head, looks me in the eye, and gives me a huge smile! I can't believe he's smiling at the vet's, with a needle stuck in his back. I think he is picking up how worried I am, and he's telling me he's OK. It is so like him to be concerned about me, and to want to comfort me, when he's the one who should need comfort.

We head home, where I sit down to relax and watch TV. I can hear Zeakie panting lying next to me. It is 8:30 p.m. I have a bad feeling, so I take Zeakie's temperature again. When I see the temperature registered on the thermometer, my heart sinks. It is close to one hundred and five. I know that convulsions and brain damage can occur at one hundred and five degrees with dogs. It is the third night of the world conference. I am not sure the emergency vet has a handle on the situation. The last emergency vet didn't know the rash on Zeak's belly was from the lymphoma. Maybe these things are too cancer-specific for the emergency vets' training. I wrestle with the decision for a few minutes, then decide I need Dr. Seiford—this is that moment—the serious emergency she gave me her number for. I decide a text will be the most unobtrusive way to reach her. I send one, describing the situation, and telling what the emergency vet had done.

Kara Seiford is in a meeting at the World Veterinary Conference when she feels the buzz of her cell phone on vibrate. She takes out her phone and holds it under the table, so as not to be seen. When she reads the incoming text, she is alarmed. Like a junior high school student sneaking a call so the teacher doesn't see it, she types in a message under the table. S-T-A-R-T P-R-E-D N-O-W!

<u>Sunday, November 6</u>

This morning the prednisone is kicking in. Zeak feels better, and his fever is down. He is eating well from lunch on. Just walking the short distance to the dam with my dogs, Allie, and Cooper; but Allie thinks even that's too much for

Zeak, so I take him home. Can't wait till Dr. Seiford is back—just two more days. We have an appointment with her Tuesday morning. I pray with all my heart that she brings back a miracle.

<u>Monday, November 7</u>

Same as yesterday, but I swear his nodes have gotten even larger. Thankfully, today is the last day of the world conference. We will be seeing Dr. Seiford tomorrow morning. Zeak lets me know he is too fatigued to take a walk.

<u>Tuesday, November 8</u>

We arrive at Animals First, check in, and sit down. In a few minutes a woman comes out of an examining room with Dr. Seiford. Dr. Seiford has her arm around the woman, who is crying. She walks the woman to the door, then she comes back and sits down next to me. We go through the usual greetings, and then I ask her what my son used to ask, when he was two and I went somewhere, and came back, "Did you bring me anything?" She gave me the answer I wanted to hear, "Yes!"

I eagerly asked her what she had found. She told me there was a new protocol out there. It was so new, that this disease had never seen it. She said that was a big reason to be hopeful. She said it was producing six-month remissions. She said that she had ordered it, and Zeak and another dog would be the first to get it here. It was being prepared and would be air-mailed in. It would arrive in seven days, on Tuesday November 15.

I told her how grateful I was to have her do this for us, especially after major surgery and losing her own dog. I told her I didn't know how she and her techs could bear the sadness they had to deal with every day, from broken-hearted pet guardians. Yet they kept their hearts open.

Then she told me that deep in her being, she knew she was supposed to do this. That it was her calling in life to do battle with this terrible disease. And that deep-seated conviction gave her the strength to go on. However, she also gave herself a break from it so it wouldn't get too overwhelming. That was why she wasn't there every day.

Then, we got to the business at hand. She was going to put Zeak back on the drug he had two weeks ago. It seemed to hold him the best. We would have to keep him on prednisone and the nausea meds, to keep him comfortable. But she was very hopeful that his new chemo could get us a second remission. She would see us next Tuesday.

As I paid our bill at the front desk, I heard the sound of a sobbing, very upset woman behind me. She was coming out of an examining room, and was crying and yelling at a man with her. From what she was saying, I surmised that she had just had her dog put down. She ran out of the building to her car. It was very unsettling. I finished our business at the front desk, and Zeak and I left.

<u>Wednesday, November 9</u>

Bill took a vacation day. It is a beautiful day, and Zeakie is up to a walk to the dam. Bill decides to join us—a rare event, and Zeakie and Lakota seem very pleased to have him along.

However, although Zeak is eating his lunch and dinner, he is starting to refuse foods he used to love, and the choices of what he can eat are dwindling. I am not going to force a huge number of pills down his throat, so I can't get most of his supplements into him. We both do the best we can do. Zeakie really tries to get what I give him down, because he knows it makes me happy, but it is getting hard. He can only eat pork tenderloin and chicken with his food mix. Everything else must either smell or taste bad to him, because he normally loves the foods he is turning down.

<u>Thursday, November 10</u>

Same as yesterday. We are limping our way to next Tuesday. It can't come quickly enough for me. I am worried about The Zeakie Dog. I do not leave him. He is panting from both the prednisone and the nausea meds, or maybe he's hot. He is lying out on the back porch a lot. Unusual—he normally stays very close to where I am, so I think he's out there to cool himself. I get an overwhelmingly sad feeling when I look at him out there, alone. Then it hits me: is he going out there to die? I have heard that animals go somewhere they can be alone when they die. It's really bothering me.

But, I decide he's hot. He is still eating a normal amount of food, just all in the second half of the day. And he still trots to the front door to greet people. I decide to get him a cooling gel mat, so he can be cool and comfortable in the house. I try to find one locally, and Donna calls everyplace she can think of. Finally, I order one to be shipped overnight—a small fortune, but really just a drop in the bucket. Only five days till he gets the new protocol.

<u>Friday, November 11</u>

Zeak is on two meds that make him pant, but the panting is bothering me, because it must be uncomfortable for him. I also still think he's hot—he still has a temperature. It's not dangerously high, but he seems so restless. I get him to lie down on the cooling mat, but he won't stay there. Instead, he has been making a place to lay right next to my chair, by laboriously moving the floor pillow. When I realize what he is doing, I help him. He is as close to me as he can get, and that's where I love him to be. He was very restless, but he seems better now, in his spot right next to me. Only four days till he gets the new protocol. And with that protocol so near, I focus all of my attention on the protocol…and I miss what I should be seeing.

<u>Saturday, November 12</u>

Same as yesterday. Still eating lunch and dinner. After dark, he goes out on the back porch again. A chill runs through me, seeing him alone in the dark, cold night. Later, he comes in and lies by my chair. I watch a little TV, and then head for bed. He is restless, and I am worried. It's only three days now. He has to make it. After I go to bed, Bill notices that Zeak cannot sleep. But he doesn't tell me that, and he doesn't wake me up. Around three a.m., Zeakie comes into my room and wakes me up. He is panting heavily, but he also seems distressed. I get up and get dressed. I get him to lie on the cool mat, and I lie on the floor next to him. He won't stay on it long. Then he throws up some thick, glue-like phlegm on the carpet. I tell him it's OK, but I am getting scared and want a vet to check him out. I leave Bill a note telling him where we are, and we get into the SUV and head for Animals First. I am very worried about Zeak's breathing, and relieved I will soon have him checked.

As we are riding in the car, I decide to sing to Zeak, in hopes that it might soothe him. I don't want to put the radio on. I need to feel more in touch with him than that. Whenever I sing and play my guitar, he always comes and lies beside me. The song that pops into my head to sing to him is an old one called, "I'll Stand by You." It was recorded by The Pretenders years ago, and it is hardly ever played on the radio any more. But I have always loved it, and it certainly fits the situation. So I sing that softly to The Zeakie Dog, all the way to Animals First.

We arrive and we go inside. I explain the situation at the front desk, and a tech comes out with a stethoscope and listens to Zeakie's breathing to see if this is an emergency, or if we can wait our turn. She determines we can wait, as I tell her his symptoms. I sit down, and Zeakie lies down be-

179

side me. There is music playing—one of the commercial-free stations that businesses can subscribe to. Then something happens that really gets my attention: The song that I was singing to Zeakie in the car—"I'll Stand by You,"* an old song that is hardly ever on the air any more—comes on. This is called a synchronicity: an event that pushes the boundaries of what can be considered coincidence. Am I getting a gentle hug to let me know everything is OK, or is this a warning? Is whatever force guides the universe trying to tell me something? If so, I wish it would be clearer in letting me know what to do.

I think about Dr. Seiford's guidelines: Zeak is still eating enough that he has not even lost weight. He still greets anyone who comes to the door. He even still does guard duty. In two days he will get the new protocol. It isn't time—not unless the vet tells me it is. But I am concerned about how uncomfortable he seems to be. How long can I let this panting go on? He woke me up for a reason. He is in distress, and is telling me that.

We wait quite a while, before we are taken in to the emergency vet's examining room. She is a familiar face, and I am very glad to see her. She is a former student of mine, and I remember how very bright she was in school, and what an animal lover she was. She listens to Zeak's lungs and says they sound "harsh." She wants to take x-rays of his lungs. I tell her that's fine, but I don't want him stressed and fighting being held down. I tell her I would rather have him sedated—even if it's dangerous—than to have him stressed when he is so ill.

She comes out with a disc, but they were not able to get great pictures. I have heard before that it's very hard to

---

*Since this writing, the song has resurfaced and has been recorded by several artists, but at this point it was obscure.

see what's going on in a dog's lungs. She says the x-rays are not diagnostic quality, but she thinks his lungs look worse—probably pneumonia, so she's putting him on a second antibiotic. She says if I want to leave him, she could put him in an oxygen tent, and it might help him breathe better. I ask her if that could be set up at home—a portable unit. She says no. I tell her I am reluctant to leave him, because it will stress him, and if something goes wrong, I don't want him to be away from the people he loves and trusts. I don't want him to die alone. She says if it were her dog she wouldn't leave him either. I tell her we only have two days before he gets a new protocol that has a good shot at putting him into remission. She does not say to me that I should consider euthanasia because my dog is suffering. I'm sure she would have told me if she thought that was the case, especially this vet. I do not ask her if she thinks that I should. If I had it to do over again I would ask her—make sure she didn't think that. But I didn't. I couldn't get the words out. And she didn't bring it up. And we only had *two days* to go.

*He was staring at me like nothing—no one—
had ever stared at me before.*

CHAPTER 36

The Beautiful Goodbye: November 13, 2011

I headed home with The Zeakie Dog and his new antibiotics. By now, the sun was up, and I was so relieved we were going home. We walked in the front door to find Bill up, and eating breakfast. Lakota was relieved and happy to see us back, and gave us both wags and kisses. I asked Bill if there was coffee, and started to take off my jacket. I say started, because Zeakie was lying down in the dining room, and what I saw in his eyes sent a shiver through me. And in that instant I *knew*…that it was over.

I knew something very wrong was happening fast, and we had to get him help, immediately. The new protocol was just forty-eight hours away, but that was too long. Zeakie had gone limp. He was struggling to get air. I could see the suffering in his eyes. And that was when I knew that I had waited too long. I had been so blinded by the hope of the new protocol that I had missed my chance to prevent this. I had done what I promised myself, and my dog, that I wouldn't do. I remembered Dr. Seiford telling me how the cancer could fill lungs with cancer cells in minutes. I knew it was happening to my dog, and I had to help him fast.

I asked Bill to get his jacket as quickly as he could, and to drive the SUV around to the back door, in case I couldn't get anyone to come to our home. I called Dr. Weaver to see if someone could come right away to put Zeak down. They were open, but could not spare anyone. I wanted Zeakie to have his last moments at home. I didn't want to move him when he was so miserable. I speed dialed the three vets on the refrigerator, but it was Sunday morning, and not one of them answered! There was no one to help us, and we couldn't wait any longer.

By then, Bill had brought the SUV around to the back gate. We helped Zeak into the back seat. He could barely move, so we lifted him using his padded seat belt harness. Not only was he weak, but some sort of partial paralysis seemed to be setting in. I put Lakota in the cargo area, and got into the back seat with Zeak. I told Bill to drive to Animals First as fast as safety would allow. It was just a bit farther than Dr. Weaver's, but the roads were faster.

I put my hand on Zeak and told him how much I loved him. I thanked him over and over for all the love and joy he had given me and others. I did not get near his face or hug him because I didn't want to restrict his air. I told him I would end his suffering as soon as I could. I could see the terrible suffering on his face, but he bore it with incredible bravery and in great dignity—more than I thought any living thing could. I told him I was so sorry—I should have ended it the day before, even if the vets didn't tell me to. If only Dr. Seiford had been there, she might have foreseen this, and helped me make the decision. But the new protocol…if I had ended it, I would have always wondered if I had done it too soon, and lost six months with him, or maybe lost a miracle. There was just no way I wasn't going to beat myself up over this for a long, long time. Watching my dog suffering, I knew what the right decision would have been. I would give anything to have saved him this suffering. I just couldn't be sure we were at the end before this happened—and neither could anyone else.

I called Elaine on my cell phone and told her briefly what was happening. She started to cry and said, "No! Not without us saying goodbye!" I told her Zeak was suffocating and suffering, and I could not wait. I suggested she grab Allie and Cooper and head for Animals First too.

Then I called Brian and told him what was coming down. He said he was too far away to make it in time. I asked him to pray for Zeakie, and he assured me he would.

Erin and John and Tundra were in their truck, heading for a barbecue at a friend's house. It was a few hours' drive, and they had just started out, headed north, when they got the call on their cell phone from Elaine. They turned their truck around and also headed for Animals First.

Then I called Animals First. I told them I was coming in with Zeakie. I told them I had just been there, that Zeakie was Dr. Seiford's patient, and that he was dying. I needed them to meet us with a gurney in ten minutes. I told them he was suffering, and pleaded with them to have everything ready to help end his suffering as quickly as possible.

When we pulled in, I was relieved to see that a gurney and two techs were waiting in the parking lot. However, the techs had no idea how to get a ninety-six pound dog out of the back seat. A vet saw us, and came down to help. He quickly thought of a way, and asked if we minded if he used the seat cover to lift him out. I said of course not—just help him, please.

As they did, Zeak tried to help, and half moved himself out, but it was obvious he had trouble moving. I looked at his face as we were walking in, and his lips were curled up like he was smiling. I was puzzled. I said to the techs, "It looks like he's smiling!" And one of the techs said, "No, he's not smiling. When dogs can't breathe they pull back their lips trying to get more air."

We were taken, with Zeak, into an examining room. A young male vet greeted us. I tried to convey the urgency of the situation to him—that my dog was suffering horribly, and would he please end his suffering quickly. He listened to Zeakie's lungs and I heard the word "harsh" again. I told him that I understood he needed to confirm his condition, and then I asked him a second time to please end Zeak's suffering as soon as he had assessed his condition. I understand that vets have a fine line to walk with euthanasia—they have to be sure the animal's owner is certain this is what they want, and won't have regrets afterward. But I could not bear to see my dog suffer like this. I was sure. My only regret was that I didn't do it sooner.

He started to explain the method they used to euthanize, and I interrupted and told him I was familiar with it—a catheter and three drugs. This time begging—I asked him to please dispense with the formalities and asked if we could please do the paperwork afterward—I thought he was talking about where the remains would be sent, and so on. But he just needed us to sign the "Consent to Euthanize" form first. I said that would be fine and scribbled my signature on it. Meanwhile, Zeak was fading fast. Soon it would be unnecessary to euthanize him.

He said that now he was going to have the techs set up the catheter to put in Zeak's leg. At that moment, everybody arrived. I told the vet I would like Zeak's human and dog friends to come in and say goodbye, while he was getting the catheter set up. He consented, and they all came in. One at a time, his human friends kneeled down in front of the gurney, so they could be at eye level, to say their loving, tearful goodbyes to The Zeakie Dog. Then, the dogs came up to Zeak. Lakota looked terrified, and sniffed Zeak frantically. Cooper came up and licked his pack leader's face. Tundra had lifted up his head and let out a cry/howl that sent chills through everyone, before he even came into the room. It was as if he knew, the minute he walked into the building, what was happening.

As soon as the vet and the techs came in, our friends and Zeak's all stepped out into the hall. Erin took Lakota for me. And then, to my astonishment, the vet told us he had to ask us to step outside while he put the catheter in. I couldn't believe my ears—I had never been asked before to leave the room while any of my other dogs were dying. I understand that some animal owners may prefer to not be present for this, but I did not want to leave my dog. However, I didn't argue because it would have made Zeak have to suffer even longer, and as I walked out the door I wondered if he thought I was abandoning him when he was dying. So someone, somewhere—perhaps even The Zeakie Dog himself—intervened, because we *should* have been together. And that was when it happened:

Out in the hall, I waited by the door and reached down to pet Lakota and comfort him. But something pulled me back up—made me stand up and look through the window in the door. That something was Zeak, who was ready to depart from his body, but would not leave without saying goodbye. The Zeakie Dog, too weak to lift his head the entire time, now had his head lifted all the way up and was facing me. He was staring at me like nothing—no one—had ever stared at me before. I actually felt myself enter some kind of altered state. In his eyes I saw terrible pain and sorrow at having to leave, coupled with the deep love he felt for me. The message was as clear as if every word had been written out. His eyes had me totally under their control, and as he stared at me, they took on a translucent quality and appeared to be moving toward me. I couldn't move…couldn't speak…couldn't breathe. I could only be there with those eyes. Suddenly all sound stopped. I was in a vacuum of silence and stillness. And then, I felt and heard a gentle little "pop!"—like a bubble bursting—and felt something pop painlessly out of my chest, from below my heart, in the center of my very core. It shot out of my body and right through the door. It stopped in the room halfway between Zeakie and me, suspended in midair. It was an orb or bubble about the size of my fist, made of clear, crystalline, brilliantly shining goo.

It was attached to me by a cord made of the same substance. It was so shiny and reflective that it took on a silvery cast. And then, the exact, identical, same thing shot out of The Zeakie Dog—also attached to him by a cord of the same substance—and collided with my bubble-orb and the two merged and became one. When that happened, a bolt of love that was so powerful it almost hurt shot down the cord into my heart. My whole body and being was filled with this incredible, powerful, love that was so strong, it was all I could do to not fall down. All of this happened very quickly, in seconds, yet seemed like slow motion. And then the vet interrupted it, opening the door and saying, "You can come in now."

I walked over to my beautiful Zeakie Dog and knelt down by his face. He lifted his head up, but now it was awkward—like a puppet being lifted by a string. I realized he was controlling his head from outside his body. He lifted his head up to kiss me. He couldn't lick me because his tongue was stuck in his mouth in the thick, glue-like phlegm that had drowned him—filled his lungs, and now totally filled his mouth. So he kissed me on the lips with his lips, just like a human would. He did this three times. Then I pulled Bill in close, and Zeakie lifted his head up for the last time, and gave Bill a human-like kiss on the lips, too.

Then the vet started the IV. "Valium," he said. "Irrelevant!" I thought—he's already out of his body. "Propofol," he said, and I held The Zeakie Dog's beautiful face between my hands. "Euthanasia," he said, lastly, and I kissed his long Zeakie nose goodbye.

I was in shock—stunned—completely changed as a human being by what had transpired in those last minutes, through the door. I was so frozen, I couldn't even cry yet. The vet opened the door, and everyone came in. Lakota and Cooper sniffed their pack leader and buddy's face, and looked grave. Tundra did not. He was a Northern Breed. Their harsh life for generations is imprinted in their genes—death was no stranger to him. He knew Zeak was no longer there.

We walked out to the front desk. The vet came out and handed me a beautiful imprint of Zeakie's paw in white clay. I thanked him, and paid the bill. Then I told them where I wanted Zeak's remains sent, where I had arranged for a private cremation to be sure his remains would be treated with respect and returned to us. We all walked out to our cars. We said our goodbyes to Erin, John, and Tundra, and Elaine, Allie, and Cooper walked us to our vehicle. I opened the back door and Lakota jumped in. Elaine and Allie gave me a hug and turned to go to their car. Before they could respond or protest, Cooper wrenched the leash from Allie's hand and jumped into the back seat, next to Lakota. He knew his friend needed him…and he needed his friend.

"It looks like Cooper will be riding with you," Allie said.

Lakota missed his brother, and would not eat his breakfast.

CHAPTER 37

Jim's Story

The next morning, Bill wanted to go to work, but walked out the door saying, "I need to see him one more time." I told him we would when we went to the private cremation. But as the minutes passed, I realized that I needed to see him too—now!

I called Animals First and thank God, the regular, loving, caring staff was there. I told them I needed to see my dog before he was picked up by the crematorium, and asked if there was time. They said there was, but to come right down because the crematorium would be picking him up soon. I called Bill, on his way to work, and he turned around and headed for Animals First too.

When we arrived, Penny was at the front desk. She came out and hugged me and said how deeply sorry she was. She told me that they had a private room for me and were bringing Zeakie in; and for me to take as much time as I needed. I told her Bill was on his way. She walked me into the room and asked if I would like her to stay with me till Bill arrived. I said that would be nice, and they brought in Zeakie's remains. To my surprise, he looked just as beautiful as always. I put my arms around him, laid my head on his thick, soft fur, and cried my heart out…and Penny cried with me. I stroked his silky ears. I knew he wasn't in that body anymore, but I loved all of him: body, emotions, mind, and spirit.

Then Bill came in, and cried his heart out, too. Despite several close human losses he had endured in his life, he said this was the hardest loss he ever had. I agreed that the same was true for me. Catherine came in, and she cried with us too. She stroked Zeakie's face, and told him she loved him. We let Lakota get up on the built-in seat so he could look at and sniff his adopted brother if he wanted to. He didn't. We stayed for over an hour, and this very busy facility generously gave us all this time in privacy with our dog, and did not rush us. There were such good, kind people here. This was an exceptional place full of exceptional people. On the way out, Dr. Seiford, who was booked solid, came over and offered her condolences and one more long, loving hug.

Just as we had decided it was time to go, the man from the crematorium arrived. I asked him to take good care of this very special dog, and he assured me he/they would. A week later, we went to the crematorium and had a private viewing of our dog for the last time. I put his favorite toys in with him and tied one of his therapy dog bandannas around his neck. A few hours later we brought Zeakie's ashes home.

The Zeakie Dog and the deep, loving connection I had—and still have—with him have changed me forever. Because of him, I have seen my own soul…and I have seen my dog's soul. Despite what you and I may have been told, I am telling you, they were one and the same—they were identical. Like most of us, I am still afraid of what I will have to go through to get out of my body, when my time here on this earth is over. But one of the many gifts Zeakie gave me is this: I am no longer afraid to die. I WILL be with my dog again. He still IS. He has made that, literally, crystal clear.

It had been several weeks since The Zeakie Dog passed and it was a beautiful, late fall day when Lakota and I went out to get the mail, and our neighbor, Jim Bosch (his real name with his permission), approached as I walked up the driveway. I stopped and turned around. Jim is the All-American Guy. He is the head engineer for media equipment for a large pharmaceutical company, our fire chief, a wonderful husband and dad; and the kind of man who, when he sees a young boy with a baseball and no one to play with, stops what he's doing to play catch with the child for a half-hour. He doesn't know I know this, but I saw him do that one day with my grandson, when I happened to look out the window.

Jim's dog, Toby, had passed away a month or two before The Zeakie Dog. He had come to offer his condolences. We talked a while about our dogs, and what a hard loss it was, and he told me he and his wife hadn't found another dog yet. I shared with him what happened when Zeak passed. He said that since I told him about that, he also had a story to share:

He went on, "A few weeks after Toby died, I was in bed trying to fall asleep when I felt a dog nose pressing on the side of my face. Then I heard a familiar thump-thud; the same familiar sound Toby always made when he lay down, because his back legs were partially paralyzed. I sat up and turned the light on… looking for something that had fallen or been knocked over. There was nothing—nothing there that could have caused that sound."

When I decided that I had to write this book, I asked Jim if I could use his story providing I changed his name and location to assure his privacy. He told me that I could use his story, and I didn't have to change anything. He said that he knows what he felt and he knows what he heard, and he stands by everything he said.

And so do I.

EPILOGUE

The Song and the Candle: After November 13, 2011

In two more days, it will be the one-year anniversary of Zeakie's passing. I cannot deny that I still miss him, terribly. I guess it "takes what it takes" to heal from a loss. Every night, after dinner, I click on the battery-operated candle on my dresser, next to Zeak's urn. Then I go back out in the living room, to begin the evening's activities. It is a ritual that comforts me. The candle has a slide switch that has no springs. In the past year, it has never failed to turn off when I turn it off. There is nothing to make it snap back, since it doesn't have a spring in the switch.

Later, before I get in bed, I turn it off, and tonight is no exception. I hear the familiar click, and then I climb into bed. I invite Lakota up onto the bed. As usual, he stares intently at "the invisible spot" for a while, before jumping up next to me. Tonight he is really fixated on it, and I have to call him three times to break him away from it, and get him to jump up on the bed.

Since I'm not ready to go to sleep, I turn on the TV and start surfing through the channels, looking for something that grabs my interest. I find something that does so, in a really big way. It is Veterans' Day, and I have happened upon a concert at the Washington Monument in D.C. A beautiful, raven-haired vocalist with an operatic voice is singing a tribute to our troops. But the song she is singing is not one of the patriotic songs that one would expect to hear at such a concert. No, she is singing a song that is such an unusual choice that it makes me sit up and take notice: a song that is an old pop song, from many years ago; a song that one rarely heard back then, and almost never hears now; a song that is not the type of song that someone with that type of voice would normally sing, especially at such a formal event.

The song is: "I'll Stand by You," by The Pretenders. It is the same song I sang to Zeakie as I drove him to Animals First, early in the morning of the day he died. It is the same song that came on the radio inside the building at Animals First, while we were waiting to see the vet. It seemed so unusual a choice for this singer at this concert that I had to wonder.

When the singer finishes, I turn off the TV. I just want to meditate in the dark and ponder if hearing that song is some kind of a signal. I can't be sure. It could just be a coincidence that I happened upon this song, so special to us. And then...I know for sure, because as I lie there, quietly in the dark, I become aware of a light in the room. I open my eyes, and to my utter amazement, the battery-operated candle by Zeakie's urn has switched itself back on.

About the Author

Margo Bowblis had never thought about becoming an author, until an experience with one of her dogs resulted in a story that had to be told. She had always owned and enjoyed dogs, but had never experienced anything like this before.

Margo received her B.A. in Fine Arts from Montclair State College in New Jersey in 1967. After graduation, she married a serviceman, and lived in California and North Carolina. When she lived in North Carolina, she became the owner of a female Labrador Retriever whom she named "Cinder." She trained and showed her, and then bred her, producing a litter of A.K.C. registered black Labrador Retrievers. From this litter, she kept a statuesque male she named "Santana" that she showed in match shows, and also trained and showed in obedience.

She returned to New Jersey when her husband was deployed to Viet Nam, and started her career as a teacher. She was an art educator for twenty-eight years. In 1989 she was the recipient of the New Jersey Governor's Teacher Recognition Award. In 1990 she was awarded a grant from the Geraldine Dodge Foundation to study the creative process. She came to the conclusion that artists can be divided into two types of creating styles: Outside-In and Inside-Out. Outside-In artists create by observing the world outside, and choosing things they wish to explore through their art.

Inside-Out artists are motivated by their inner thoughts and emotions, and they look for ways to express them directly or symbolically.

After retiring from public education, Margo focused her attention on painting, sketching, singing and playing her guitar in coffee houses, and renewing her passion for animals. She and her dogs, Lakota and Zeak, have all been active, working volunteers with a therapy dog organization. Through a friend, she learned about the work of therapy dogs, and had her dogs trained and certified for this work, logging over one hundred visits to sick and elderly people.

She has a son, Thomas Lapenter, Jr., a daughter-in-law, Patricia Lapenter, and a grandson, Thomas Lapenter III, who reside in New Jersey. Margo also resides in New Jersey with her husband William, Lakota, and the spirit of The Zeakie Dog.

Zeak, canine friend Ellie, the author, Lakota, and Shy

ART AND PHOTOGRAPHY CREDITS

Illustrations, photography, and cover design by the author with the following exceptions:

- Snow-covered trees on the cover by William Bowblis

- Studio portaits by Demitrius of Infinity Photography
  574 Newark Pompton Turnpike, Pompton Plains, NJ 07444
- (973) 256-4000
  www.infinity8photo.com
      Lakota on page 60
      Zeak on page 182
      About the Author
      Back cover photograph

- Last photo in book by Laurie E. Krauss

www.ingramcontent.com/pod-product-compliance
Lightning Source LLC
Chambersburg PA
CBHW062057290426
44110CB00022B/2627